ON FASCISM

ON FASCISM

12 Lessons from American History

Matthew C. MacWilliams

ST. MARTIN'S
GRIFFIN

NEW YORK

First published in the United States by St. Martin's Griffin, an imprint
of St. Martin's Publishing Group

ON FASCISM. Copyright © 2020 by Matthew C. MacWilliams.
All rights reserved. Printed in the United States of America. For
information, address St. Martin's Publishing Group, 120 Broadway,
New York, NY 10271.

www.stmartins.com

Library of Congress Cataloging-in-Publication Data is available
upon request.

ISBN 978-1-250-75269-7 (trade paperback)
ISBN 978-1-250-75270-3 (ebook)

Our books may be purchased in bulk for promotional, educational,
or business use. Please contact your local bookseller or the
Macmillan Corporate and Premium Sales Department at
1-800-221-7945, extension 5442, or by email at
MacmillanSpecialMarkets@macmillan.com.

First Edition: 2020

10 9 8 7 6 5 4 3 2 1

For Susan Glasheen and Margaret MacWilliams
Throughout their lives, they persisted!

When fascism came into power, most people were unprepared, both theoretically and practically. They were unable to believe that man could exhibit such propensities for evil, such lust for power, such disregard for the rights of the weak or such yearning for submission.

—Erich Fromm, *Escape from Freedom*

Fellow citizens, we cannot escape history.

—Abraham Lincoln (December 1, 1862)

AUTHOR NOTE

If you love the promise of America and our Enlightenment aspirations as much as I do, coming to terms
with our failures and confronting their root cause is
an essential step toward rejecting authoritarianism
and attaining a robust *e pluribus unum* (out of many,
one) steeped in the power of equality, diversity, and
democracy.

That is the America I seek, and the reason behind
writing this book.

Those who won our independence believed . . . that fear breeds repression; that repression breeds hate; that hate menaces stable government.

—Justice Louis Brandeis,
Whitney v. California (1927)

Please, I can't breathe.

George Floyd, final words (2020)

INDEX OF AMERICAN
AUTHORITARIAN ATTITUDES

DEMOCRACY

46% of Americans are inconsistent supporters of democracy and democratic institutions*

34% of Americans agree it is more important to follow the will of the people today than the principles laid out in the U.S. Constitution

31% of Americans agree that having a strong leader who does not have to bother with Congress and elections is a good way of governing the United States

---

* All data in this section (except this item) compiled from American Survey Research Project's "Three National Panel Surveys" fielded in the United States on October 2016, March 2017, and July 2017 by YouGov. This item is from: "Follow the Leader, Exploring American Support for Democracy and Authoritarianism," Democracy Fund Voter Study Group, accessed June 9, 2019, https://voterstudygroup .org/publication/follow-the-leader. ASRP is a fiscally sponsored project of the Proteus Fund that is directed by Dr. Matthew C. MacWilliams. Co-investigators on the surveys are Dr. Brian Schaffner (Tufts University) and Dr. Tatishe Nteta (University of Massachusetts Amherst).

24% of Americans agree with limiting the freedoms of the press and media in the United States

13% of Americans agree that if it is necessary to protect our country, the president should limit the voice and vote of opposition parties

OTHERING

30% of Americans agree with the statement "I often find myself fearful of other people of other races"

16% of Americans agree an ideal society requires some groups to be on top and others to be on the bottom

14% of Americans agree some groups of people are simply inferior to other groups

AGGRESSION AND THREAT

44% of Americans agree that increasing racial, religious, and ethnic diversity represents a threat to the security of the United States

23% of Americans agree that sometimes other groups must be kept in their place

15% of Americans think that those who disagree with the majority are a threat to the interest of the country

RACISM AND SEXISM

31% of white Americans say black Americans are somewhat to very violent

28% of Americans agree that many women are actually seeking special favors, such as hiring policies that favor them over men, under the guise of asking for "equality"

26% of white Americans say black Americans are somewhat to very lazy

CONTENTS

ON FASCISM

INTRODUCTION

POGO KNOWS

We have met the enemy, and he is us.
                                    —Pogo

The Index of American Authoritarian Attitudes is my tool for estimating the gap between the universal values, beliefs, and attitudes Americans are reputed to hold and our actual commitment to democratic principles and ideas.

The results are eye-popping.

While the Declaration of Independence says "that all men are created equal," 14 percent of Americans think that some groups of people are simply inferior to others. We assume that the Constitution and the rule of law are essential governing precepts, yet 34 percent of Americans say it is more important to follow the will of the people today than the constitutional principles on which the rule of law stands. Thirty-one percent of Americans agree that having a strong leader who does not have to bother with Congress and elections is a good way to govern the United States. And 13 percent of Americans say we should junk the Bill of Rights and let the president limit the voice and vote of opposition parties if the country is threatened in any way.

The data in the index comes from national surveys taken in the United States between 2016 and 2017. They reveal attitudes that are inconsistent with what so many know or think they know about our fellow Americans. For example, 26 percent of white Americans think black Americans are somewhat to very lazy; 27 percent are more likely to say Hispanic Americans "do not share my values." Thirty-six percent think Muslim Americans are somewhat to very violent. And when it comes to equality of opportunity, 42 percent oppose the notion that all groups in America should have an equal chance to succeed, or feign neutrality on the issue.[1]

How do we square these opinions with the story of American exceptionalism and the values that ostensibly anchor it? We must start by recognizing that these findings are a symptom of something deeper—an underlying disposition that has been with America throughout its history. That disposition is authoritarianism.

Approximately 18 percent of Americans are highly disposed to authoritarianism. Another 23 percent or so are attitudinally just one step below them on the authoritarian scale. When these two positions are taken together, roughly four out of every ten Americans tends to favor authority, obedience, and uniformity over freedom, independence, and diversity. (A more detailed explanation of how "authoritarianism" is estimated is discussed in Appendix 3.)

When fear or circumstance, inflamed by the rhetorical misrepresentations of a would-be autocrat, activate the authoritarianism latent in these Americans, many of them will sacrifice liberty for security. They will side with the strongman and other purveyors of tyrannical majoritarianism, choosing to escape from freedom rather than defend it.[2]

Their activated, unyielding support for a strongman can become a new identity that provides a sense of belonging, generates social and material benefits, and delineates group boundaries for its members to patrol, enforce, and defend. In its most virulent expression, when the benefits of division and othering (identifying a particular group as intrinsically different and potentially threatening) exceed those of unity of people and purpose, this process of group identification, aggression, and protection can spiral into fascism.

Our fervent belief in the myth of American exceptionalism persuades us that we are uniquely immune to the activation of authoritarianism. Some of us contend that we are different from people in every other country in the world.

We are not.

To understand one of the root causes of polarization in America today, set aside the fairy-tale story of American history. Our ancestors were not magically cleansed of their disposition to authoritarianism upon alighting on the shore of Plymouth Plantation, being dragged off a slave ship in Savannah harbor, or disembarking on Ellis Island. Fascism may be a twentieth-century foundling birthed by Mussolini's Fasci de Combattimento, but its taproot, authoritarianism, is a disposition that is as old as humanity itself. Like smallpox and other Old World diseases that ravaged the native populations in the New World, authoritarianism migrated with the first settlers to America.

Since America's founding, there's been a perpetual tug-of-war between our aspiration toward a more perfect union and the authoritarian impulses that have coursed through our polity and politics. These two competing forces—and the differing visions of America they yield—have been with the nation since the founding. Take, as one example, the Civil War period (1861–1865). Abraham Lincoln represents the more enlightened view of equality and fundamental human rights. "I am naturally anti-slavery," Lincoln wrote in 1864. "If slavery is not wrong, nothing is wrong. I cannot remember when I did not so think, and feel."[3] The antithesis of Lincoln at the time was Roger Taney, the chief justice of the Supreme Court from 1836 to 1864. His decision in the *Dred Scott* case (which decided that black people, enslaved or free, were not entitled to U.S. citizenship) exemplified authoritarian othering in action. Writing for the Court's majority in *Dred Scott v. Sandford*, Taney asserted that blacks are "beings of an inferior order . . . so far inferior, that they had no rights which the white man was bound to respect."[4] To Chief Justice Taney, the "equality for all" principle embedded in the Declaration of Independence was limited to whites. At least Taney did not pay lip service to the Declaration's enlightened aspirations, as so many Americans do today.

The ongoing tug-of-war between those (like Taney) who are disposed to authoritarianism and those (like Lincoln) who are not courses through our history. It overwhelms the better angels of our nature and produces the dirty laundry at the bottom of America's historical hamper. It provokes America's ugliness and too often produces the shameful stories that stain our history. And it reveals our predilection for what James Madison called the "infection of violent passions."

In Federalist 63 (the 85 Federalist papers were written by Madison, Hamilton, and Jay in support of ratification of the U.S. Constitution), Madison warned:

> There are particular moments in public affairs when the people, stimulated by some irregular passion, or some illicit advantage, or misled by the artful misrepresentations of interested men, may call for measures which they themselves will afterwards be the most ready to lament and condemn.[5]

American history is littered with these Madisonian moments. Times in which the rights of minorities (or whatever group was being "othered") were trampled. Events when the rule of law was bent to justify lawbreaking (e.g., the 1919–20 Palmer Raids, which we will examine in Lesson 8). Periods when almost any means or act was judged acceptable if it led to the attainment of a desired end—no matter how antithetical *the end* was to the ideals of the Constitution and the rule of law.

What a nation believes about its past is at least as important as what the past actually was.

—Benjamin Carter Hett, *The Death of Democracy*

The Alien and Sedition Acts of 1798, the Indian Removal Act of 1830, Chinese exclusion, the internment of Japanese Americans, and the return of Jim Crow under the guise of law and order[6] are just a few of these moments of which Madison warned.

These Madisonian moments are not historical relics. In today's America, where an increasing number of us are "bowling alone"—to use the term political scientist Robert Putnam applies to a United States in which civic organizations are in steep decline—hate groups have increased 30 percent from just four years ago and now number more than a thousand.[7] They are an unparalleled sector of uncivil civic growth in twenty-first-century America.

Our nation's egalitarian, democratic aspirations have always competed for supremacy with a darker, pathological tradition rooted in authority, obedience, and the hegemonic enforcement of majoritarian interests and norms. This is a journey that began at our founding. Who are the "we" in "we the people"? What does "all" mean in "all men are created equal"? In the beginning, "all" and "we" were exclusive and codified. They referred to white male property owners, and no one else. Yet the Declaration of Independence and the preamble to the Constitution are certainly not dry legal recitations of rights. They are soaring, revolutionary proclamations—audacious statements of hope and aspiration that are the responsibility of each generation to protect and perfect.

The odds of reaching a more perfect union and living up to our democratic ideals improve if we remove our blinders and examine the history too many refuse to acknowledge. That important journey begins by going to the core of America's origin myth—the notion that Americans are some special breed of people—and debunking it. Our inheritance may be unique, but we as a people are not. Not even in the beginning. As the turn-of-the-century sociologist Samuel G. Smith noted in his speech at the First International Eugenics Congress, held in London in 1912, "As to the criminally born, England knew what to do with them: she sent them to America to found the first families of New York or Virginia."[8]

You might be disposed to dismiss the latent authoritarianism residing in our country, and its repeated expression throughout our history, as anomalous—the proverbial exceptions that prove our fundamental commitment to equality. You might argue that throughout history, the Enlightenment ideals at the core of our democracy have always prevailed. And according to most American history textbooks, you would be more or less right.

But have these ideals been secured or just tempo-
rarily won? Is American history moving inexorably
toward a more perfect union, as sociologist Gunnar
Myrdal and political scientist Louis Hartz maintained in the mid-twentieth century, or is our future
less certain? Are the voting rights of women, blacks,
Asians, Hispanics, and Native Americans safe, or are
they at risk today? Is the safety of Jews and Muslims ensured or not? Was the "separate but equal"
doctrine definitively overturned by *Brown v. Board
of Education*, or has it morphed into something just
as destructive? Was Jim Crow extinguished, or has it
been replaced by something new and just as harmful?
And at the center of these and other pressing questions: Are American democracy and its constitutionally protected institutions as robust and safe as many
of us assume?

Consider the evidence before us. In the last few
years, many Trump administration nominees to federal district and circuit courts have refused under
oath in Senate Judiciary Committee hearings to af-
firm the landmark 1954 Supreme Court ruling in
Brown vs. the Board of Education (at the time, the
high court ruled 9–0 in its favor). If today's judicial
appointees can't be relied upon to vocally repudiate
the racist construct of "separate but equal," then every
precedent, every legal advancement toward a more
perfect union is now on the chopping block.

In 1989, after the Berlin Wall fell and the Cold
War ended, political observers, led by American philosopher Francis Fukuyama, proclaimed that the "end

of history" was nigh. Democracy had defeated communism. According to Fukuyama, free-market liberalism and globalism, tethered to democratic national and supranational institutions, were evolving into "the final form of human government."[9] No process existed that could take democracies backward. Today that declaration seems farcical. But even then, in the irrational exuberance following the fall of communism, Fukuyama should have known better. Because a core lesson from history, acknowledged by political philosophers since the days of Athens and Sparta, is that democracy is fragile.

The founders of the United States knew this lesson well. As future president John Quincy Adams wrote in a letter in 1814, "Democracy never lasts long. It soon wastes, exhausts, and murders itself. There never was a democracy yet, that did not commit suicide."[10] The issues that concerned the founding generation of Madison, Jefferson, Hamilton, and Franklin have burned hot and challenged our country throughout its history. And they remain with us today. As political scientists Karl D. Jackson and Giovanna Maria Dora Dore wrote two months before Trump's general election victory in 2016:

> Democracies remain fragile for political reasons, not because of social class or culture clash, but because democracies contain within themselves substantial population blocs which are either ambivalent about democracy or opposed to it, and these groups, under particular circumstances and with the *right*

leadership can be mobilized to weaken or destroy democracy.[11]

The American authoritarian is one of those population blocs whose activation is a gateway drug to the demise of democracy. In America today, according to survey work done by the Democracy Fund Voter Study Group, only a slight majority of citizens (54 percent, to be exact) are consistent supporters of democracy.[12] The inconsistent supporters of democracy—many of the other 46 percent highlighted in the first item on the Index of American Authoritarian Attitudes—think having a strong leader who doesn't pay attention to election results or Congress is a good way to run a government. They don't think it's very important to live in a country that is democratically governed.[13]

They are wrong.

There are now ample warning signs that authoritarian-minded Americans have been activated by fearmongering and othering rhetoric, and that the powerful democratic norms and institutions that in theory exist to combat such forces are fraying and threadbare. The question before us all is: Can we stop the rot?

American history is riddled with examples of moments when authoritarian fascism and its concomitant pathologies were ascendant—instances when too many Americans either obeyed or looked the other way. In the chapters that follow, I will examine twelve of these examples, explain their relevance, and extract the historical lesson each one teaches. Applying these lessons to our civic life is how Americans can resist the siren call of authoritarianism and perfect our democracy.

More than two hundred years ago, leaving Independence Hall on the final day of the convention that produced the Constitution of the United States, a bystander asked Benjamin Franklin what type of government the delegates had created. Franklin's answer: "A Republic, if you can keep it."[14]

Franklin's cautionary response is as pertinent today as it was then. Our answer now depends on how well and quickly we recognize the authoritarian awakening that is today reshaping America, and how we can rise up to stop it.

Denial will not save American democracy, but coming to terms with our history might.

Can freedom become a burden, too heavy for a man to bear, something he tries to escape from?

—Erich Fromm, *Escape from Freedom*

LESSON 1

AMERICA ENLIGHTENED
OR AUTHORITARIAN?
LINCOLN VS. DOUGLAS

> We hold these truths to be self-evident, that
> all men are created equal.
> —Declaration of Independence

While the Declaration of Independence's pronouncement that all men are created equal is etched into the consciousness of most Americans, arguments over what these words mean have raged throughout our history. The items in the "Othering" section of the Index of American Authoritarian Attitudes demonstrate that the disagreement over the meaning of "created equal" continues to this day.

The debate comes down to some simple questions. Who is in, and who is out? What does "all" mean? And, as a corollary, does "men" mean only straight white men, or any human regardless of race, ethnicity, gender, or sexual orientation?

One of the most important public debates over the meaning of the Declaration's clarion statement of equality came to a head in Illinois in 1858 during the campaign for United States Senate between Abraham Lincoln and Stephen Douglas. At the time, Lincoln was a former state legislator and congressman with a law practice in Springfield. He joined the newly formed Republican Party and was selected as the party's general election candidate for Senate. Douglas was the incumbent Democratic senator from Illinois. During the run-up to the 1858 election, Lincoln and Douglas faced off in a series of seven debates held across the state. Douglas won the Senate contest against Lincoln but lost the presidential election to him two years later.

14% of Americans think some groups of people are simply inferior to others.[1]

During the debates, Douglas argued that the Declaration applied to whites only. Lincoln disagreed. The competition between their two visions of equality is a Rorschach-test illustration of the contest of values and ideas at the heart of American history.

The 1858 campaign for Senate in Illinois was framed by the Supreme Court's decision a year earlier in *Dred Scott v. Sandford*. Writing for the Court's 7–2 majority, Chief Justice Roger Taney asked:

> Can a negro, whose ancestors were imported into this country, and sold as slaves, become a member of the political community formed and brought

into existence by the Constitution of the United States, and as such become entitled to all of the rights, and privileges, and immunities guaranteed by that instrument to the citizen?

Taney's answer, and the Court's pronouncement, was no. Slaves could not become citizens. But Taney wasn't done. The Court also ruled that Congress could not prohibit the spread of slavery to the territories—proto-states that stretched approximately from the Mississippi westward. The Missouri Compromise, enacted by Congress in 1820 (congressional legislation that preserved the status quo balance of power between free and slave states by admitting Maine to the union as a free state and Missouri as a slave state, while banning slavery in all northern Louisiana Purchase states), was thus unconstitutional because, as the legal logic concluded, slaves were the property of their owners and that property could not be taken without due process.

Justices John McLean and Benjamin R. Curtis disagreed with Taney and the Court's majority. Curtis's dissenting opinion, published in Boston before the majority opinion in *Dred Scott* was finalized, skewered Taney's arguments. Curtis wrote:

It has been often asserted that the Constitution was made exclusively by and for the white race. It has already been shown [earlier in the dissent] that in five of the thirteen original States, colored persons then possessed the elective franchise, and were among those by whom the Constitution was ordained and established. If so, it is not true, in point of fact that the Constitution was made exclusively by the white race. And that it was made exclusively for the white race is, in my opinion, not only an assumption not warranted by anything in the Constitution, but contradicted by its opening declaration, that it was ordained and established by the people of the United States, for themselves and their posterity. And as free colored persons were then citizens of at least five states, and so in every sense part of the people of the United States, they were among those for whom and whose posterity the Constitution was ordained and established.[2]

Taney was furious, and a nasty feud broke out between them. A few months later, Curtis resigned from the Court.

Two days before Taney's opinion in *Dred Scott* was announced, James Buchanan was sworn in as the fifteenth president of the United States. In his inaugural speech, Buchanan, a Democrat who lobbied the Court behind the scenes and was given a heads-up by Taney of the impending decision, praised the upcoming ruling. After the ruling was announced, he declared that slavery in the territories was constitutionally protected.

The *Dred Scott* decision inflamed the newly formed Republican Party, whose central organizing principle was to stop the spread of slavery. A year later, in 1858, at the Republican state convention in

Springfield, Lincoln accepted the party's nomination for Senate by declaring: "A house divided against itself cannot stand."[3]

The Senate contest between Republican Lincoln and Democrat Douglas was set. It would be, in large part, a campaign over the meaning of America's founding documents. Would Illinois voters choose white supremacy and slavery or embrace equality as a universal value and reject slavery as an affront? As Lincoln warned in his acceptance speech:

> Either the opponents of slavery, will arrest the further spread of it, and place it where the public mind shall rest in the belief that it is in course of ultimate extinction; or its advocates will push it forward, till it shall become alike lawful in all the States, old as well as new—North as well as South.[4]

Douglas's argument for slavery began with a repudiation of Lincoln's interpretation of the Declaration of Independence and Constitution. Like Chief Justice Taney, President Buchanan, and southern leaders like former vice president and senator John C. Calhoun, Douglas asserted that America's founding documents were written solely to establish the rights and privileges of whites.

16% of Americans agree that an ideal society requires some groups to be on top and others to be on the bottom.[5]

Equality between races was a chimera. Whites were superior and would always be so. Slavery was a natural outcome of this natural order. In a speech delivered in Chicago, Douglas's unvarnished racist view of America rang clear: "This government of ours is founded on the white basis . . . for the benefit of the white man, to be administered by white men."[6]

Furthermore, Douglas accused Lincoln of fomenting civil war and extolled the Supreme Court's decision in *Dred Scott*. Lincoln spoke in Chicago the day after Douglas's racist harangue. The speech was Lincoln's boldest statement to date on equality:

> Let us discard all this quibbling about this man and the other man—this race and that race and the other race being inferior, and therefore they must be placed in an inferior position. . . . Let us discard all these things, and unite as one people throughout this land, until we shall once more stand up declaring that all men are created equal. . . . I leave you, hoping that the lamp of liberty will burn in your bosoms until there shall no longer be a doubt that all men are created free and equal.[7]

As historian Eric Foner noted in his book *The Fiery Trial*, Lincoln, "in opposition to Douglas's racialized definition of American nationhood . . . counterposed a civic nationalism grounded in the ideals of the Declaration of Independence. Not race or ethnicity but principle bound Americans to one another."[8]

This exchange between Lincoln and Douglas

occurred before the seven debates for which the 1858 Senate campaign is so well known. The debates were held across Illinois in the fall of 1858. They focused on slavery and the meaning of equality. Voters in Illinois went to the polls afterward.

Republicans won the statewide vote in the election by a 50 percent to 47 percent margin over the Democrats and Douglas. But Lincoln was not elected to the Senate. The Seventeenth Amendment to the Constitution, providing for the direct election of U.S. senators by popular vote, was still fifty-five years away. The Senate race in Illinois (and in every other state in the Union until 1913) was decided by a vote in the state legislature.

Like the Electoral College, which has elected as president the candidate who lost the popular vote in four U.S. elections (1876, 1888, 2000, and 2016), the selection of senators by legislative vote was designed as a constitutional check on popular will. In Illinois, gerrymandering and population shifts during the 1850s led to the overrepresentation of rural Democrats in state legislative races. The result: while Republicans won the popular vote by 3 percentage points, Lincoln lost the Senate election in the Illinois legislature by a vote of 54 to 46.[9]

CODA

Abraham Lincoln's view of slavery was absolute. Slavery was evil: "If slavery is not wrong, nothing is wrong."[10] His attitude toward equality was not.

Speaking in Peoria in 1857, Lincoln said that the authors of the Declaration

> intended to include all men, but they did not intend to declare all men equal in all respects. They did not mean to say all were equal in color, size, intellect, moral development, or social capacity. They defined with tolerable distinctness, in what respect they did consider all men created equal—equal in "certain inalienable rights, among which are life, liberty, and the pursuit of happiness.[11]

From our perspective today, this qualified view of equality is surprising. But it captures only part of Lincoln's vision of America, the Declaration of Independence, and the Constitution. Lincoln continued:

> They meant to set up a standard maxim for free society, which should be familiar to all, and revered by all; constantly looked to, constantly labored for, and even though never perfectly attained, constantly approximated, and thereby constantly spreading and deepening its influence.[12]

To Lincoln, equality was an aspiration—something to be looked to and labored for. Lincoln's Senate campaign was part of that labor. His defeat paved the way for a successful campaign for president in 1860. His advocacy for equality and Douglas's campaign against it are part of the historical tug-of-war between America's othering impulses and Enlightenment ambitions. Like Lincoln, neither the Constitution nor the Declaration of Independence is perfect. They are aspirational documents whose interpretation and application are an open question and often contested. Perfecting them is our responsibility.

In 1858, Illinois voters chose Lincoln and a forward-looking vision of America. Illinois's systematically skewed legislative caucus chose Douglas and a regressive view of America's values and liberties. Though the words *authoritarianism* and *fascism* had not yet been coined, the constitutional mechanisms intended to insulate democracy from popular will led to the selection of othering inequality over the aspirational Enlightenment values on which America was founded. Ironically, the Electoral College produced the same undemocratic outcome in 2016 as the Republican Party turned its back on Lincoln's legacy and became the party of Trump.

31% of white Americans today are more likely to agree that black Americans are somewhat to very violent.[13]

LESSON 2

FOMENTING FEAR

INAUGURATION DAY 2017
AND THE PARANOID STYLE

Throughout American history, social elites, religious purifiers, media opportunists, and wannabe political strongmen—on both the right and the left—have used the tools of fear and conspiracy to stir the violent passions of which Madison warned in Federalist 63. Historian Richard Hofstadter dubbed this instrumental fearmongering "the paranoid style in American politics" and described it as an "old and recurrent phenomenon in our public life" that "has a greater affinity for bad causes than good" and "has been frequently linked with movements of suspicious discontent."[1]

Mashed up, Madison's theory and Hofstadter's historical observations yield an important insight about the use and power of fear in American politics: Since the founding of our Republic, paranoid politicians have employed "artful misrepresentations" to activate the authoritarianism latent in many Americans.[2]

27% of Americans claim that the "deep state" definitely exists.[3]

The political path to awaken American authoritarianism is well worn. First, purveyors of the paranoid style conjure an other—typically a minority group that is politically weak, distinct, and vulnerable. Second, this other is described as different from mainstream Americans, and identified as a clear and present threat to majoritarian values and traditions. Third, a paranoid leader stokes fear that a hidden conspiracy or outright revolution to undermine mainstream values is afoot and alleges that the other is behind it—activating American authoritarians. Finally, in its most virulent manifestation, growing fear of the other is manipulated to rationalize actions that violate fundamental values, norms, laws, and constitutional protections guaranteed to all Americans.

Fear breeds repression: that repression breeds hate; that hate menaces stable government.
—Justice Louis Brandeis, *Whitney v. California* (1927)

The paranoid leader transforms the other into an existential threat and wields this threat to justify the junking of the rule of law and the unrestrained exercise of power. To Hofstadter, American history was chock-full of examples of the paranoid style at work—for instance, Timothy Dwight's jeremiad against the "false doctrines" of Masonic societies and the Illuminati (titled *The Duty of Americans, at the Present Crisis*). Dwight was president of Yale at the time he delivered his diatribe on Independence Day 1798. He warned that the Masons and Illuminati were conspiring with Democratic-Republicans to overthrow the Federalists and God's "kingdom."[4] Soon after his sermon, "the pulpits of New England," infected by Dwight's conspiratorial vision, "were ringing with denunciations of the Illuminati, as though the country were swarming with them."[5]

Conspiracy theories about the Pope's designs on the United States, what Hofstadter labeled Puritan porn, merged with a growing fear of immigrants and became a recurrent theme of the paranoid style of politics in America for more than one hundred years.[6] From the supposed Jesuit plot, uncovered in the 1830s, to install a "scion of the House of Hapsburg . . . as Emperor of the United States" to Jesuit missionaries allegedly "prowling about all parts of the United States in every possible disguise expressly to ascertain the advantageous situations and modes to disseminate Popery," fears of Catholicism and Catholic immigrants infested American politics.[7]

By the 1840s, anti-Catholic, nativist movements, which would coalesce into the American Party and become known as the Know-Nothings, battered politics and politicians across America, including Abraham Lincoln. Lincoln shared his alarm over the nativist bile

of the Know-Nothing Party in a letter to his close friend
Joshua Fry Speed, writing:

> I am not a Know-Nothing. That is certain. How
> could I be? How can anyone who abhors the op-
> pression of Negroes, be in favor of degrading
> classes of white people? Our progress in degeneracy
> appears to me to be pretty rapid. As a nation, we
> began by declaring that "all men are created equal."
> We now practically read it "all men are created
> equal, except negroes." When the Know-Nothings
> get control, it will read "all men are created equal,
> except negroes, and foreigners, and Catholics."[8]

Nativism and the "secret cabal of the international
gold ring" became staples of paranoid politics after
the Civil War.[9] Socialism was added to the paranoid
style's gallery of rogues at the turn of the century. And
after World War II, Senator Joseph McCarthy fully
weaponized Red-baiting, mainlining communist conspiracy theorizing into the bloodstream of American
politics. McCarthy declared, "When a great democracy is destroyed, it will not be from enemies from
without, but rather because of enemies from within,"
and then waved a "list of 57" names of people working in the State Department who he claimed were
communist sympathizers.[10]

Stoking fears of a Catholic conspiracy to sabotage
the United States remained an on-again, off-again
tool of the paranoid style of politics until well after

the turn of the twentieth century. The nomination of four-term New York governor Al Smith, a Catholic, as the Democratic candidate for president in 1928 signaled the beginning of the end of anti-Catholicism as a political weapon. But it wasn't until the election of America's first (and only) Catholic president—John F. Kennedy in 1960—that the attack was completely defanged. In that election, political fearmongering about Senator Kennedy's fealty to the Vatican fell mostly on deaf ears. The political utility of targeting Catholics as a threatening other had finally run its course, but the paranoid tactic of using religious differences to stoke division and fear was not discarded, just transformed.

Pat Buchanan, the Republican politician and pundit who once claimed to be more Catholic than the Pope, offered a new other on which paranoid politicians could feast—the so-called cultural libertines of the left. "There is a religious war going on in this country," Buchanan warned in his address to delegates at the 1992 Republican National Convention. "It is a cultural war as critical . . . as was the Cold War itself, for this war is for the soul of America."

Today Muslims, immigrants, alleged deep-state conspirators, and "libtards" (the epithet coined by conservatives that fuses *liberal* and *retard* into one cudgel) round out the many targets paranoid leaders deride and attack as threats to the real America.

Hofstadter's dissection of the message and modus operandi of the paranoid spokesman is a powerful tool for understanding how the underbelly of American politics is activated. And it reads like an outline of President Donald Trump's 2017 inaugural address. Hofstadter writes, "The paranoid spokesman sees the fate of this conspiracy in apocalyptic terms—he traffics in the birth and death of whole worlds, whole political orders, whole systems of human values."[11]

In his address, Donald Trump warns of "mothers and children trapped in poverty in our inner cities; rusted-out factories scattered like tombstones across the landscape of our nation, an education system, flush with cash, but which leaves our young and beautiful students deprived of all knowledge; and the crime and gangs and drugs that have stolen too many lives and robbed our country of so much unrealized potential."[12]

Hofstadter writes, "Since what is at stake is always a conflict between absolute good and absolute evil, what is necessary is not compromise but the will to fight things out to the finish."[13]

Donald Trump proclaims, "This American carnage stops right here and stops right now."[14]

Hofstadter writes, "Since the enemy is thought of as being totally evil and unappeasable, he must be totally eliminated."[15]

Donald Trump says, "We will reinforce old alliances and form new ones—and unite the civilized world against radical Islamic terrorism, which we will eradicate completely from the face of the Earth."[16]

Hofstadter writes, "The paranoid's interpretation of history is distinctly personal: decisive events are not taken as part of the stream of history, but as the consequences of someone's will."[17]

Donald Trump says, "We assembled here today are issuing a new decree to be heard in every city, in every foreign capital, and in every hall of power. From this day forward, a new vision will govern our land. From this moment on, it's going to be America First."[18] And as if cued by Hofstadter, Trump proclaims, "Safety will be restored. . . . I am the law and order candidate."[19]

* * *

Richard Hofstadter obviously never met Donald Trump. He never attended one of Trump's "Make America Great Again" rallies. But he studied Trump's political forebearers thoroughly and viewed their fearmongering, grievance-stoking, and othering politics as a clear threat to American democracy.

Hofstadter's account of the paranoid style in politics is a cautionary tale illuminating the workings of a political malaise repeated throughout American history. It is a political strategy Americans must recognize and reject.

CODA

Trump's triumph in 2016 represents a modern high-water mark of the paranoid style. Fear-stoked politics is at its zenith. It has evolved. And it is activating authoritarianism in American politics in a way not seen before.

It is the job of all Americans today—whether they come at politics from the left, right, or center—to identify the purveyors of paranoid-style conspiracy claptrap and ignore them. This is a tall order, but the future of our democracy depends on it.

Twenty-seven percent of Americans have already bought completely into the deep-state delusion pushed by the paranoids. Another 47 percent say the deep state "probably exists." America's future hangs in the balance.

LESSON 3

ALL LIES MATTER

THE FATHER OF HATE RADIO AND DEEP-STATE CONSPIRACIES

James Madison and his fellow revolutionaries recognized that demagoguery—the stoking of violent passions and prejudices to obtain power—and its handmaiden, conspiratorial fearmongering, were an inevitable threat to democracy. In the critical moments when a demagogue stirred public passions, Madison counted on the great expanse of the nascent Republic as well as the Senate to protect the people from themselves. The Senate, a "temperate and respectable body of citizens," was designed to check the power of a demagogue's rhetoric by suspending "the blow mediated by the people against themselves until reason, justice, and truth . . . regain[ed] their authority over the public mind."[1]

The sheer scope of America, with "people spread over an extensive region," would insulate the Republic from the "infection of violent passions" by a demagogue and make the "factious combinations" they strove to build less likely.[2] Madison did not use the phrase "authoritarian activation" to describe the demagogue's stoking of violent passions in Federalist 63; the term *authoritarian* would not appear in the English language for approximately another one hundred years. And the insight that authoritarians could be activated by threats real or imagined was another two hundred or so years down the pike. Yet the notion that a self-interested and preternaturally irresponsible leader could use rhetoric, falsehoods, and insults to whip people into a mobocracy that demanded unjust measures was a central concern of America's founders.

From "the history of the petty republics of Greece and Italy," which "were kept in a state of perpetual vibration between the extremes of tyranny and anarchy," Madison knew that a mob, or a leader empowered by the mob, could secure the power to "run roughshod over even the institutions created to preserve their freedoms."[3]

46% of Trump voters and 17% of Clinton voters agreed that the Clinton campaign emails made public by WikiLeaks contained messages about sex trafficking and pedophilia.[4]

While the founders thought they understood human nature, they could not anticipate how, over time, well-intentioned reforms and institutional erosion would weaken some of the protections they had so carefully crafted to protect the Republic. They could not foresee how the great geographic expanse of the United States would become an irrelevant barrier to the call of the demagogue in a digital world of 24/7 production and consumption of "information." The idea that 81 percent of Americans would have a smart-phone in their back pocket, instantaneously connecting them to the world and wannabe demagogues to them, was beyond their predictive powers.[5] For all their in-sight and pragmatism, they could not design a fail-safe system to thwart those whose illiberal impulses and need for power continually threaten democracy.

The geographic bulwark protecting America from self-interested demagogues did not collapse all at once, but its demise was accelerated, starting in the 1920s, by the advent of commercial radio. In 1926, NBC established a radio network that spanned vast swaths of the United States. That October, Catholic priest Charles Coughlin, who would later be labeled the "Father of Hate Radio," aired his first broadcast on WJR-AM in Detroit.[6]

From the start, Father Coughlin's broadcasts on WJR were wildly successful. Focusing on religious content, Coughlin built his hour-long show and its membership adjunct—the Radio League of the Little Flower—into a marketing behemoth. After the stock market crash of 1929, the content of Cough-lin's *Golden Hour* began a steady transformation, becoming less religious and increasingly dedicated to the discussion of political and social ills and how to solve them.

Coughlin's dark, conspiratorial worldview fit the

times to a T. He was suspicious of "modernism and radicalism," sure that these "insidious forces were in a malignant stage" and "beginning to permeate" America.[7] His mission was to organize a counterrevolution to stop them.[8]

In late 1930, Coughlin moved his broadcasts to the CBS radio network, whose sixteen stations had the potential to reach 40 million people each week— about one out of every three American citizens at the time. By 1931, Father Coughlin had become a national celebrity. Major magazines profiled him; newspapers ran regular stories reporting on his sermons, and the church picnic he sponsored for children in the spring of 1931 drew almost 20,000 people.

As his popularity grew, so did the acerbity of his rhetoric. Warning of hidden conspiracies and attacking radicals, socialists, and communists turned out to be good radio. It expanded Coughlin's listening audience and increased donations to his church. So in 1931, with the Great Depression in full swing, Coughlin added a new target to his list of conspirators: international bankers.

The phrase "international bankers" is a well-known dog whistle—conspiracy theorists' code for Jews. The use of the term was popularized by the book *The Protocols of the Elders of Zion*, which is conspiracy hatemongering in its vilest form. A Russian fabrication first published in 1903 and thoroughly debunked just a few years later, the book purported to reveal the secret details of a Jewish conspiracy, including Jewish bankers, to take over the world.

Father Coughlin blew the international banker dog whistle repeatedly on his radio show, and CBS responded by not renewing his contract; NBC also refused to sell him time on its network. Undaunted, and with the support of the Catholic Church and his bishop (*The Golden Hour* was producing lots of cold hard cash for the diocese during a difficult economic time), Coughlin bought radio time directly and grew his own network to twenty-seven stations. By the time Franklin D. Roosevelt began campaigning for the presidency, Coughlin's radio empire was in place and its content was no longer bound by the standards of CBS.

In the 1932 election, Father Coughlin attacked Hoover and backed Roosevelt. However, Roosevelt spurned him the year after the election. Shut out of mainstream politics by party leaders on both sides of the aisle, Coughlin organized the National Union for Social Justice in 1934 to fight for social change and prepare the way for a new political party to contest the 1936 presidential election. By 1935, Coughlin claimed that 13.5 million Americans had joined his organization. If the established political parties would not make room for Coughlin inside their tents, he would use his microphone to build his own.

By 1935, Coughlin had become "dangerously important" and a "mob leader," according to his contemporary biographer Ruth Mugglebee. Some may "scoff at the anti-capitalist, anti-bank, anti-international league views of Father Coughlin," she warned, "but they cannot laugh off easily the acceptance by millions of his home-spun doctrines, political, economic, and social."[9]

Producing a radio show is infinitely easier than starting up and running a political party. With the new Union Party racked by internal divisions and constrained by media gatekeepers, Coughlin's candidate for president in 1936, William Lemke, lost miserably, garnering only 892,000 votes.[10] (Roosevelt won with nearly 28 million votes. Republican Alf Landon took second with 16.5 million.)

His party in tatters, Father Coughlin returned to the radio—again with the support of the Catholic Church, which considered him an effective opponent of communism. This time, however, Coughlin's rhetoric and actions grew into full-blown, conspiratorial anti-Semitism.

He accused Jewish bankers of supporting the Russian Revolution, and he formed an organization called the Christian Front. The Christian Front became known for "beating up Jews on the streets of American cities and proclaimed themselves to be 'Father Coughlin's brownshirts.'"[11]

Coughlin's magazine, *Social Justice,* doubled down on his anti-Semitic crusade by publishing excerpts from *The Protocols of the Elders of Zion.* Coughlin's recycling of the thoroughly debunked *Protocols* demonstrated the depth of his anti-Semitism and the lengths he would go to attract an audience by stoking fear and attacking a vulnerable minority.

In November 1938, a week after Kristallnacht—the infamous Night of Broken Glass, when Jews and their homes, businesses, and institutions were attacked by Nazis in Germany and Austria—Father Coughlin crossed a rhetorical Rubicon. With millions of Americans listening to his *Golden Hour*, he blamed the Jews for the Kristallnacht wilding. According to Coughlin, the Nazis were not responsible for the killing and mayhem. Rather, they had to strike because "communism and Judaism are too closely woven for the national health of Germany."[12] A Gallup poll taken a month later found that 22 percent of Americans had heard Coughlin's broadcasts during November.[13] By comparison, today conservative commenter Sean Hannity's average weekly radio audience comprises about 4.6 percent of Americans, while progressive Thom Hartmann reaches around 2.2 percent.[14]

Eventually, Coughlin's Nazi sympathizing, hate-mongering rhetoric, and Christian Front vigilantes became too much for his backers in the Catholic Church. Following the installation of Pope Pius XII in 1939, the Vatican began to curtail Coughlin's activities. By 1940, his radio scripts had to be vetted by church censors. A year and a half later, *Social Justice* was banned by the U.S. Post Office because of its incendiary speech and Nazi sympathies. Coughlin's days as the Father of Hate Radio were soon over.

With his celebrity, Charles Coughlin blazed a conspiracy-theorizing trail that many have since followed. But Coughlin pushed his fearmongering in an analog world patrolled, albeit imperfectly, by mainstream society's gatekeepers: editorial boards, political parties and interest groups, government, the law, academe, professional associations, and religious institutions. Known as the "guardrails of democracy," these gatekeepers developed, maintained, and enforced unwritten norms and conventions that have bolstered the Constitution and republican government in America. In today's 5G digital world, they have lost much of their informal power.

Like most evolutions, the fall of democracy's gatekeepers and the concomitant democratization of media and information have benefits and costs. But one outcome of the transformation from analog to digital poses a particular threat to Madisonian democracy. Without gatekeepers, there is little to stop Coughlin clones—amplified by bots and trolls, foreign and domestic—from feeding unsuspecting Americans a steady diet of conspiracy theories, fear, and "alternative facts."

The political opportunity presented by unmoderated digital communications is every demagogue's dream. The business model of digital media makes clickbait conspiracy theorizing very lucrative. The result is a media landscape that markets fear and conspiracies while exacerbating societal divisions.

Nothing demonstrates the menace posed by the brave new digital world to democracy better than the 2016 general election campaign conspiracy hallucination known as "Pizzagate." It began with a crime: the hacking of the Democratic National Committee's servers, the stealing of private emails, and the packaging and release of those emails by Russian propaganda cutout WikiLeaks. WikiLeaks' timing of its email dumps was geared to hurt Clinton and help Trump. But no one in either campaign (or in the Kremlin, for that matter) could have anticipated how conspiracy theorists on Reddit, 4chan, and other dark corners of the web would transform internal Clinton campaign emails into "proof" that the campaign's leadership, along with other Democratic insiders, was running a child sex ring from the basement of a local pizza shop in Washington, DC—called Comet Ping Pong—in their spare time.

Like a virus, the lie about Democrats being involved in child sex trafficking spread from Reddit's hub for Trump supporters across the web to the conspiracy website Infowars, Twitter, alt-right activists, demi-demagogues, wannabe muckrakers, and (oddly enough) supporters of Turkish president Recep Erdogan. Overseas bots and Russian propagandists joined in to amplify the rumor, creating a conspiracy echo chamber that fooled a significant number of Americans in a surprisingly short time.

Spawned by WikiLeaks, the fake news fantasy of Democratic pedophiles using Comet Ping Pong as the base for a child sex ring spread far and wide across the cybersphere. Then, it took a dangerous real-world turn. A man from North Carolina became so upset that he took his gun, got in his car, drove to Washington, and raided the pizza joint to free the children allegedly shackled in its basement.

But there were two problems. First, Comet Ping Pong does not have a basement. Second, no Clinton or Democratic child sex trafficking operation exists. It was all a political hoax geared to inflame Americans and inflict damage on Democrats. The gullible gunman, who stormed through the door of Comet Ping Pong carrying an AR-15 rifle, pled guilty to assault with a deadly weapon. Fortunately, no one was killed.

CODA

In 1770 John Adams, acting as a defense attorney for the British soldiers allegedly involved in the Boston Massacre, opined, "Facts are stubborn things, and whatever may be our wishes, our inclination, or the dictates of our passion, they cannot alter the state of facts and evidence."[15]

Facts may be stubborn, but when self-interested partisans and demagogues deny the importance of facts and relentlessly assert alternative versions of reality, discerning fact from fiction becomes exceedingly difficult.

All lies matter. Lies are an accelerant whose constant and repeated use speeds the demise of democracy. Almost 250 years after Adams asserted the primacy of facts, the importance of the truth to democratic debate and policymaking is no longer a given. Manufactured facts, designed to aid and abet the production of desired political outcomes, are deployed without hesitation or remorse. Entrepreneurial authoritarians use so-called alternative facts to shape reality to their advantage, and then justify their falsifications as necessary and no big deal.

"Facts are white noise," said the British business-man Arron Banks to Donald Trump. Banks had spent nearly $11 million of his own money promoting deceptive advertising with the aim of winning the Brexit vote. "Sometimes . . . you're going to say things, and sometimes you don't have all the facts to back it up," asserted former Trump campaign manager Corey Lewandowski, defending his boss's ceaseless prevarications.[16] President Trump's counselor Kellyanne Conway proclaimed to a national audience on *Meet the Press* that false claims about the size of the president's inauguration crowd were simply "alternative facts." Conway's bald-faced dissembling gobsmacked the program's host, Chuck Todd, one of the few remaining gatekeepers in America, who responded: "Alternative facts aren't facts, they are falsehoods."[17]

Alternative facts and conspiracy-mongering pose a clear and present danger to American democracy—especially when the lies and conspiracy theories are swallowed hook, line, and sinker, and then repeated for political gain by those who know better. As Fiona Hill, a former top adviser to President Trump on Russia and Europe, clearly warned us during her testimony on November 21, 2019, during the House Intelligence Committee's impeachment hearing: "Based on questions and statements I have heard, some of you on this committee appear to believe that Russia and its security services did not conduct a campaign against our country—and that perhaps, somehow, for some reason, Ukraine did. This is a fictional narrative that has been perpetrated and propagated by the Russian security services themselves."[18]

In his landmark analysis of the rise of Nazism in Germany, psychologist Erich Fromm cataloged the dangers of debate and decision-making in the absence of facts or in spite of them. He wrote, "We are dealing here with a political system which, essentially, does not appeal to rational forces of self-interest, but which arouses and mobilizes diabolical forces in man which we had believed to be nonexistent, or at least to have died out long ago."[19] In this system, "facts lose the[ir] specific quality . . . each fact is just *another* fact. . . . [Man becomes] bewildered and afraid and just goes on gazing at his little meaningless pieces" of facts.[20] When facts lose meaning, the ability to think critically is paralyzed and democracy dies.

The paranoid style of politics and the demagogues who practice it have a new and dangerous outlet in the digital sphere. It exacerbates the political and social divisions in America and blocks the way to our strongest and most exceptional aspiration—*e pluribus unum*.

LESSON 4

GAGGING THE PRESS, QUASHING DISSENT

SEDITIOUS LIBEL, 1798

On November 2, 1799, the indictment was issued. The charge: seditious libel.

The alleged perp was Thomas Cooper, editor of the *Sunbury and Northumberland Gazette*—a man Thomas Jefferson called years later "the greatest man in America."[1]

The indictment read as follows: "Thomas Cooper . . . being a person of a wicked and turbulent disposition designing and intending to defame the President of the United States and to bring him into contempt and disrepute and to excite against him the hatred of the good people of the United States . . . wickedly and maliciously did write, print, utter, and publish a false, scandalous, and malicious writing against the said President of the United States."[2]

The evidence was a broadside in which Cooper had dared to criticize the policies of President John Adams. Cooper questioned Adams's "sanction[ing of] the abolition of trial by Jury in the Alien law"

[and the] "entrench[ment of] his public character behind the legal barriers of the Sedition law."[3] In the
trial that followed, the United States alleged that Cooper's words violated the Sedition Act passed by the
Federalist-controlled Congress in July 1798.

24% of Americans agree with limiting the freedoms
of the press and media in the United States.[4]

The Sedition Act was the first U.S. statute to crim-
inalize free speech. It was enacted by Federalists to
quash dissent and gag the increasing opposition to
their hegemony. Drawing from the English legal tradition of criminalizing "seditious libel," Section 2 of
the act made it a crime for any person to "write, print,
utter, or publish" or to "knowingly and willingly as-
sist or aid in writing, printing, uttering, or publishing
any false, scandalous and malicious writing or writ-
ings against" the government, Congress, or the president.

Speech that was defamatory or contemptuous, that
"excite[d] . . . the hatred of the good people of the
United States," that "stir[red] up sedition within the
United States," or that aided "any hostile designs of any
foreign nation against the United States" was illegal.[5]
Questioning the Federalists and their governing majority was now a crime. The free speech provisions of
the Bill of Rights—guaranteeing in the First Amendment that "Congress shall make no law . . . abridging
the freedom of speech, or of the press"—had been

ratified for just seven years when Federalist supporters of the Sedition Act argued that it "only protected
writers from the government's [prior] restraint of
publication."[6] Once published or uttered in the public
square, speech was no longer sacrosanct.

The Sedition Act was the product of a deeply divided
country—the eighteenth-century version of today's political polarization. On one side were the Federalists,
led by President John Adams and Alexander Hamilton.
On the other side were Vice President Thomas Jefferson, James Madison, and the Democratic-Republicans,
who believed that self-government was possible only
when speech and the press were free.

In 1798, however, the Federalists were in the
majority. In an attempt to lock in their partisan
advantage—an authoritarian go-to-strategy—they
passed the Sedition Act and several other bills.[7]

Twenty-six Americans were arrested for violating
the Sedition Act.[8] At least ten went to trial. Most of
them were Democratic-Republican journalists, including one whom historian Bruce A. Ragsdale, the
director of the Federal Judicial History Office, described as "the editor of the most influential opposition newspaper in the nation."[9] Everyone who went
to trial was convicted by juries packed with Federalist
supporters and overseen by Federalist judges. The fix
was in.

Democratic-Republican congressman Matthew
Lyon from Vermont was the first target. While running
for reelection, Lyon accused Adams of "an unbounded
thirst for ridiculous pomp, foolish adulation, and

selfish avarice." He was summarily arrested, convicted, and jailed for seditious libel. From his jail cell, Lyon continued campaigning and became the first candidate for Congress to win reelection while behind bars.

Thomas Cooper's trial was rigged just like Matthew Lyon's. In a courtroom presided over by Samuel Chase, a Federalist-appointed associate justice of the Supreme Court, Cooper did not stand a chance. In front of the jury, Chase accused Cooper of "poisoning the minds of the people," praised the Sedition Act, and even added to the prosecutor's bill of particulars against Cooper.[10] Cooper countered with a defense that fell on deaf ears but included this astute observation: "I know that in England the king can do no wrong, but I did not know till now that the President of the United States had the same attribute."[11]

When the case was turned over to the jury for judgment, they deliberated at a nearby tavern and reached a guilty verdict in less than an hour. Cooper was sentenced to six months in jail and a $400 fine.

In the preface of his account of the trial, which was published before the verdict, Thomas Cooper asked the public to consider an important question:

> Reader, when you have perused this trial, shut the book, and reflect. I dare not state the conclusions with which it is pregnant, but which must force themselves with melancholy conviction on your mind: ask yourself however, is this a fair specimen of the freedom you expected to derive, from the

adoption of the Federal Constitution? And whether the Men who can sanction these proceedings, are fit objects of reelection?[12]

Cooper's questions are as pertinent today as they were more than 200 years ago.

CODA

First Amendment protections of speech and the press seem airtight. But in practice, the application of these constitutional tenets has been anything but absolute—especially when all three branches of the federal government are controlled by one faction. The use of the Sedition Act to quash dissent and imprison dissenters is a cautionary tale of what is possible when political power is unchecked and runs roughshod over the Constitution and the rule of law.

The Sedition Act of 1798 expired on March 3, 1801. The question of whether the act violated the intent of the First Amendment was never considered. The establishment of judicial review was two years in the future. (The Supreme Court's landmark decision in *Marbury v. Madison* asserted the judiciary's exclusive power to interpret the Constitution. As Chief Justice John Marshall wrote in the opinion, "It is emphatically the duty of the Judicial Department to say what the law is.")

If a Sedition Act case had somehow made it onto the docket of the Supreme Court before the law expired, however, the outcome in front of a Court stuffed with Federalists was uncertain. Freedom of speech and the press might have been gutted not only by the Federalist Congress and the president but also, for years to come, by America's third branch of government, led by the Supreme Court.

LESSON 5

TAKING WHAT IS
RIGHTFULLY OURS

AMERICA'S *LEBENSRAUM* AND THE
"TREATY" OF NEW ECHOTA, 1835

The first treaty between the United States and the Cherokee Nation was signed in Hopewell, South Carolina, in 1785. Over the next fifty years it was followed by fifteen more, often negotiated under duress. Each treaty promised peace and took Cherokee property while guaranteeing that the remaining land would be forever Cherokee. The guarantees were worthless. European immigrants, now citizens of the United States, brazenly ignored each treaty by forcibly seizing Cherokee land. State governments joined in, refusing to protect Cherokee property and challenging Native American sovereignty. The federal government's response was to look the other way.

We beg leave to observe and remind you that the Cherokees are not foreigners but original inhabitants of the United States; and that the states by which they are now surrounded have been created out of land which was once theirs.[1]

—The Cherokee Nation to
Secretary of War John C. Calhoun

The process was inexorable. White European immigrants wanted more land. Natives owned it. Instead of enforcing the law, white lawmakers sided with the white lawbreakers.

The rule of law was no match for the American *Lebensraum*. (*Lebensraum* is a German concept meaning the living space needed for a particular people or nation to thrive. Hitler adapted the concept to justify the territorial expansion of Nazi Germany.) Europeans spread across Native American lands that became, by force and decree, the United States. The emerging American society and its institutions deemed Native Americans inferior to white immigrants. Native Americans were simply an other, beyond the protective penumbra of the law.

For a nation founded by property owners and pledged to protect property rights, the wholesale appropriation of sovereign Native American land is a cautionary tale of how malleable laws are when those with power in a society label members of a minority group as inferior human beings.

37% of Americans today oppose following treaties made with Native Americans by the United States

government, including agreements that give Native
Americans control of their own land.[2]

The last treaty written while the Cherokee still
possessed land in Georgia, North Carolina, Tennessee, and Kentucky was the Treaty of New Echota.
The story of its negotiation and ratification by the
U.S. Senate is a shameful demonstration of what can
occur in America when the rule of law collides with
unbridled presidential power and the immoral assertion of group dominance over an other.

The treaty led to the forced removal of Cherokees
from their land to "Indian country." Known today as
the Trail of Tears, this genocidal act left thousands
of Cherokee dead and most of those who survived
destitute.

This is a history we cannot and must not forget.

* * *

Beginning in the 1780s, the federal government
pursued two contradictory policies toward Native
Americans. While working to purge them from their
sovereign land, the government also encouraged Native Americans to acculturate. The Cherokee fought
removal, but adapted readily to white cultural norms.
By the turn of the century, many farmed and engaged
in trade and commerce. They were educated by Protestant missionaries, who also served up religious
training. In July 1827, the Cherokee Nation adopted
a constitution modeled after that of the United States,

specifying a government with legislative and judicial branches and a chief elected by the legislature. The first chief was John Ross. Less than a year later, the nation began publishing its own newspaper, the *Cherokee Phoenix*. The Cherokee acculturated so completely that John C. Calhoun, then vice president of the United States, warned President Jackson's cabinet that the cultural progress of the Cherokee could pose a real barrier to efforts to remove them.[3]

As the Cherokee became more law-abiding and "civilized" (according to the standards of Anglo-American culture), white immigrants regularly broke the law by encroaching on Cherokee land and stealing it. In large part, the federal government ignored this constant appropriation of Cherokee property, refusing to remove whites who seized land from the Cherokee even though the government was required to do so by the Trade and Intercourse Act of 1802. Defying federal law, southern state governments also encouraged white colonization of Cherokee land. Federal inaction and state defiance of federal treaties transmitted an unmistakable message to white immigrants: Cherokee land was theirs for the taking. President Jackson considered these illegal seizures an indirect but effective way to attain his ultimate goal—forcing Native Americans from their land. As Jackson remarked to a congressional ally: "Build a fire under them [Cherokee]. When it gets hot enough, they'll move."[4]

A year or so after the Cherokee constitution was enacted and John Ross was elected tribal chief, the governor of Georgia turned up the heat by signing

a bill on December 28, 1828, that seized all Cherokee land and placed it and members of the Cherokee
Nation under the legal jurisdiction of the state. The
unstated reason behind the state's sweeping action:
whites had discovered gold on Cherokee land.

Even though the Georgia legislation contravened
federal law and violated the Constitution's supremacy clause ("all Treaties made . . . under the Authority of the United States shall be the supreme Law of
the Land"), the federal government again did nothing. President Jackson ignored the Constitution and
sided with Georgia, arguing that state power over Indian affairs, when exercised within state boundaries,
superseded federal law. Then he went even further.
In his first annual message to Congress, delivered on
December 8, 1829, Jackson publicly called for the removal of all "Indians beyond the white settlements."
The legislative vehicle for accomplishing this policy
was the Indian Removal Act of 1830. Aware of what
today would be dismissively labeled as the "snowflake" concerns of many in the public and Congress,
Jackson, during his campaign to secure passage of
the Removal Act, soft-pedaled how the ethnic cleans-
ing of Native Americans would be accomplished. He
suggested, "This emigration [the removal of Native
Americans] should be voluntary, for it would be as
cruel as unjust to compel the aborigines to abandon
the graves of their fathers, and seek a home in a distant land." At the same time, he acknowledged that
"our conduct toward these people" will reveal "our
national character."[5]

Jackson's high-minded happy talk whitewashed his real intentions. The Indian Removal Act would give the federal government the leverage it needed to force Native Americans from their lands. As Jackson said privately: "You must get clear of them [Cherokee and other Native Americans] by legislation. Take judicial jurisdiction over their country; build fires around them, and do indirectly what you cannot do directly."[6] What Jackson meant by "do indirectly what you cannot do directly" was steal the land, possessions, and livestock of the Cherokee and any other Indian nation that stood in the way of white *Lebensraum* in America. The Indian Removal Act and the treaties it enabled through force, fraud, or both were a means to an end. To Jackson, and many Americans who came both before and after him, taking Native American land by manipulating democratic institutions and constitutional law was simply a social application of what would later become known as Darwin's law of natural selection.

Many in Congress doubted whether Jackson would deal fairly or humanely with Native American tribes. Their concerns grew when an internal War Department memorandum was leaked, detailing plans to bribe and intimidate the tribes into moving. Even so, the Indian Removal Act of 1830 passed the Senate easily. And when its passage in the House of Representatives came into question, Jackson's bullying secured a narrow but winning margin of 102 to 97.

The final language of the act guaranteed "that nothing in this act contained shall be construed as authorizing or directing the violation of any existing treaty between the United States and any of the Indian tribes" and that tribes "may choose to exchange the lands where they now reside." This assuaged the misgivings of some members of Congress and the consciences of many others. But Jackson had no intention of following existing treaties or giving Native Americans a choice in the matter. *Lebensraum* was now federal policy.[7]

* * *

The immorality at the very core of the Removal Act was not lost on American leaders such as Henry Clay. Writing to Daniel Webster in the weeks after its passage, Clay warned that the bill "threatens to bring a foul and lasting stain upon the good faith, humanity, and character of the nation."[8] Clay's concern was prescient.

Three barriers to removal remained, however. First, the Cherokee had sued to protect their treaty rights; federal court rulings could stymie Jackson's plans. Second, the Jackson administration needed to conclude a new treaty with the Cherokee in which they agreed to move, and the treaty had to be ratified by the Senate. Finally, the federal government needed to deport the Cherokee to Indian country. Physically moving thousands of Cherokees from Georgia to what we know today as Oklahoma—a journey of more than 900 miles—was no small undertaking.

Chief John Ross and his lawyer William Wirt, a

former attorney general of the United States, filed suit in federal court to nullify Georgia's violation of Cherokee sovereignty and enforce the tribe's existing treaty with the United States. The case, *Worcester v. Georgia*, was decided by the Supreme Court in March 1832.

In the 5–1 decision, written by Chief Justice John Marshall, the Court ruled that the Cherokee Nation "is a distinct community occupying its own territory . . . in which the laws of Georgia can have no force, and which the citizens of Georgia have no right to enter but with the assent of the Cherokees themselves, or in conformity with treaties and with the acts of Congress. The whole intercourse between the United States and this Nation [the Cherokees], is, by our Constitution and laws, vested in the Government of the United States." In essence, the Court ruled that the Cherokee Nation was a sovereign nation with its own laws. Relations between the nation and the United States were regulated by treaty and, under the supremacy clause of the Constitution, could not be nullified by a state law. Federal treaties guaranteed the Cherokee (and other Indian nations, for that matter) "their original natural rights as the undisputed possessors of the soil."[9]

The ruling required that Georgia respect Cherokee sovereignty and release Samuel A. Worcester, a missionary who was helping the Cherokee and had been arrested by state authorities. Georgia refused to do either. Once again, President Jackson sided with the state. Ignoring the Constitution's supremacy clause and the Supreme Court's authority, Jackson refused to enforce the Court's decision.

The Court was left with a ruling it could not implement. The United States was left with a constitutional crisis caused by a president who refused to enforce the law. And the Cherokee were left with a just decision that was unjustly ignored. In a letter to fellow justice Joseph Story, Chief Justice John Marshall wrote, "I yield slowly and reluctantly to the conviction that our Constitution cannot last."[10]

The first barrier to Jackson's plan had been surmounted by ignoring the Supreme Court and the Constitution. But there was a cost: Jackson's flagrant disregard for the rule of law was threatening the constitutional foundation of the nation.

28% of Americans agree that the power of federal courts to declare executive orders of the president unconstitutional should be eliminated.[11]

Jackson's next task was persuading the Cherokee to voluntarily sign a treaty to abandon their land. The Cherokee Chief John Ross refused. So Jackson went around him: through bribery and threats, Jackson's treaty commissioner, J. F. Schermerhorn, forced a minority faction of the Cherokee to agree to a new treaty, delivering the so-called arrangement that Jackson demanded.

The agreement—the Treaty of New Echota—was

a complete fraud. The federal property appraiser assigned to the Cherokee knew it and told the secretary of war that the "treaty is no treaty at all, because it [was] not sanctioned by the great body of the Cherokees and [was] made without their participation or assent. . . . The delegation taken to Washington by Mr. Schermerhorn had no more authority to make a treaty than any other dozen Cherokees accidentally picked up for that purpose. I now warn you and the President that if this paper of Schermerhorn's called a treaty is sent to the Senate and ratified you will bring trouble upon the Government and eventually destroy this [Cherokee] nation."[12]

Even so, the treaty was submitted to Congress, and on May 18, 1836, by a one-vote margin, the Senate ratified it. Five days later, Jackson signed the treaty into law. The document gave the Cherokee two years to vacate their homes. Two years later, with few Cherokees willing to obey the fraudulent treaty and abandon their land, the federal government moved in and began rounding them up, deporting them by forced march to Indian country.

The first-person accounts of what General Winfield Scott, the officer in command of the deportation effort, called the "clearing" of Cherokees are sickening. As one soldier who witnessed the Cherokee removal wrote, "[I] have seen men shot to pieces and slaughtered by thousands, but the Cherokee removal was the cruelest work I ever knew."[13] Another observer wrote:

The Cherokee are nearly all prisoners. They had been dragged from their houses. . . . In Georgia, especially, multitudes were allowed no time to take anything with them, except the clothes they had on. Well-furnished houses were left a prey to plunderers, who, like hungry wolves, follow in the train of the captors. These wretches rifle the house, and strip the helpless, unoffending owners of all they have on earth. Females, who have been habituated to comforts and comparative affluence, are driven on foot before the bayonets of brutal men. Their feelings are mortified by vulgar and profane vociferations. It is a painful sight. The property of many has been taken, and sold before their eyes for almost nothing—the sellers and buyers, in many cases having combined to cheat the poor Indians. . . . Many of the Cherokees, who, a few days ago, were in comfortable circumstance, are now victims of abject poverty.[14]

By the time the removal campaign was complete, Martin Van Buren was president. He was quick to spin the truth. In his second annual address to Congress, Van Buren said that Cherokee had been removed "without any apparent reluctance" and that the process produced the "happiest effects."[15] Decades later, Teddy Roosevelt praised the use of national power against Native Americans "in favor of the hard-pressed wilderness vanguard of the American people." At the same time, Roosevelt recognized that these white settlers "speedily s[a]nk almost to the level of their barbarous foes" and "barely considered an Indian as a human being."[16] And today, even the Supreme Court's highly respected justice Stephen Breyer falls into the trap of minimizing the horrific removal of Cherokee from Georgia to Oklahoma on the Trail of Tears. Breyer writes, "This sad story [the Cherokee removal] has a few positive aspects. Despite the tragic outcome, it helped establish a principle—namely, like cases need to be treated alike."[17] This is a judge's view of the legal ramifications of *Worcester v. Georgia*, but it is this type of compartmentalizing that we must not allow to whitewash and obfuscate the inhumanity of our ancestors' actions.

CODA

The removal of the Cherokee and other Native American tribes is an abject, systemic failure of American democracy and the rule of law. All of our hands are dirty—those who lived in the past and those who enjoy the fruits of the American *Lebensraum* today. Denying this fact, reframing it, or minimizing it is dangerous. The destruction visited on the Cherokee is not a "sad story." It is a shameful part of our history that we must remember and never repeat.

* * *

President Jackson ignored the law and recklessly abused his power. The nascent federal bureaucracy enabled him. Congress looked the other way. The Supreme Court was feckless. "Thanks be to God," wrote Justice John Story to his wife, "the Court can wash their hands clean of the iniquity of oppressing the Indians and disregarding their rights."[18] And soldiers did what they do well—they followed orders.

A president who places himself above the rule of law, and institutions, sycophants, and toadies who look the other way and enable him, corrode the very fabric of our constitutional system and what truly makes America a place of promise and possibilities.

Of all the paintings available to him, President Donald Trump chose the portrait by Ralph E. W. Earl of Old Hickory, Andrew Jackson, to hang next to him in the Oval Office. The choice is unsurprising.

LESSON 6

USING FEAR AND VIOLENCE
TO CONTROL AND
SUBORDINATE OTHERS
THE UNITED STATES OF LYNCHERDOM

Four thousand seven hundred and forty-two Americans were murdered by mob violence between 1882 and 1968.[1] At least, that is the number of lynchings documented by researchers who scoured historical accounts and reported their findings in Section 2 of the Justice for Victims of Lynching Act. The act was proposed in 2018 by Cory Booker, Kamala Harris, and Tim Scott—the sole black members of the United States Senate.

While 4,742 murders is a staggering number, it represents only the murders verified by researchers. Other lynchings, private affairs where white vigilantes strung up their victims away from the scrutiny of reporters and record-keepers, have gone unrecorded.

Lynching was a tool used by whites to terrorize black Americans. The Equal Justice Initiative defined it as an instrument "for maintaining racial control by victimizing the entire African American community, not merely punishment of an alleged perpetrator for a crime."[2] It was widespread, brutally lawless, and often committed in public to emphasize the ultimate power whites held over blacks. Most of the people lynched were black. Most of the lynchings occurred south of the Mason-Dixon Line. But mob murder was not solely a southern pathology. It occurred in all but four states.[3]

Edward Coy was tied to a tree, tortured, and burned to death in front of a crowd of 15,000 in Texarkana, Arkansas.[4] In Paris, Texas, 10,000 watched as Henry Smith "was placed on a scaffold . . . securely bound . . . tortured for fifty minutes by red-hot iron brands thrust against his quivering body . . . placed against him inch-by-inch until they were thrust against the face. Then . . . kerosene was poured on him, cottonseed hulls placed beneath him, and [he was] set on fire."[5] Two hundred white citizens lynched Richard Neal in Shelby County, Tennessee.[6]

In Roseland, Louisiana, Meredith Lewis was acquitted by a white jury of wrongdoing but lynched anyway.[7] And in Decatur, Illinois, Samuel Bush was lynched for drinking water from a white person's well. He was stripped naked and hanged from a telegraph pole. The perpetrators were well known in the community. At first, twenty-two of them were indicted for the crime. But all the indictments were eventually dropped. Not a single one "suffered a whit more inconvenience for the butchery of [Bush], than they would have suffered for shooting a dog."[8]

Nearly all the people who perpetrated lynchings

were never punished for their crimes.[9] Not because the crimes were carried out in secret or the perpetrators were unknown. Many of the perps were community leaders, elected officials, and police officers. These well-known public figures went unpunished because the concept of equal justice under the law was rejected by local, state, and federal officials. Lynchings were a vicious means white society used to attain a specific end—the renewed social control of blacks in post-Reconstruction America. As Senators Booker, Harris, and Scott noted in 2018, "Lynching succeeded slavery as the ultimate expression of racism" in the United States.[10]

For more than four decades, lynching was a common occurrence. In the 1880s and 1890s, more than one hundred lynchings were reported each year (except in 1890).[11] The high-water mark for murder-by-mob during this time was 230 dead in 1892. That year, Ida B. Wells, a former slave turned journalist, published her first book, *Southern Horrors: Lynch Law in All Its Phases*. It was followed in 1895 by *A Red Record: Tabulated Statistics and Alleged Causes of Lynching in the United States 1892–1894*. Wells's work, the reporting of the Tuskegee Institute, and an increasing number of newspapers and magazines like *The Nation* exposed lynching for what it was and remains today: America's national crime.[12] Despite the growing national awareness of lynching, the crime was largely ignored by the federal government. It was considered, quite conveniently, a state matter rather than a federal concern. President Theodore Roosevelt was in office for nine months before he cautiously referenced it. At Arlington National Cemetery on Memorial Day 1902, as he dismissed the raging criticism of the army's crackdown on Filipino insurgents, Roosevelt made this elliptical reference to lynchings: "From time to time there occur in our country . . . lynchings carried on under circumstances of inhuman cruelty and barbarity—cruelty infinitely worse than any that has ever been committed by our troops in the Philippines."[13]

This brief public mention of lynching by Roosevelt was applauded by black newspapers and opinion leaders. At least Roosevelt had mentioned the crime and identified it as a barbarity.[14] Four years later, however, Roosevelt was still talking about the problem instead of taking action.

Lynching occupied six paragraphs of Roosevelt's 1906 State of the Union address.[15] In those paragraphs, he called "the attention of the Nation . . . to the epidemic of lynching and mob violence that springs up, now in one part of our country, now in another." He asserted that "the crime is peculiarly frequent in respect to black men." Then, blaming victims of lynchings for their deaths, he argued that "the greatest existing cause of lynching . . . [is] the perpetrating, especially by black men, of the hideous crime of rape." According to Roosevelt, black Americans were lynched more than whites because black men were more likely than white men to rape white women. Lynching was not a question of race, racism, or racial subordination; it was a question of criminal behavior on both sides. "There is no question of 'social equality' or 'negro domination' involved; only the question of relentlessly punishing bad men," argued Roosevelt. Lynching was hideous, but so was the rape of white women, and "every colored man should realize that the worst enemy of his race is the Negro criminal."[16]

The rape excuse was a common justification for lynching—a get-out-of-jail-free card racists regularly played to rationalize racial terrorism. It was a lie, of course, disproven time and again. Nonetheless, it was a lie repeated by white society and leaders to justify lynching as a necessary response to a brutal crime perpetrated by black men. For example, a month after Roosevelt's 1906 State of the Union address, Senator Benjamin R. Tillman declared from the floor of the U.S. Senate, "As governor of South Carolina I proclaimed that although I had taken the oath of office to support the law and enforce it, I would lead a mob to lynch any man, black or white, who had ravished a woman black or white."[17]

Tillman did much more than lead a lynch mob. A few years earlier, as governor, Tillman turned over an innocent man under his legal protection, John Peterson, to a South Carolina mob. Peterson was accused of rape but had a solid alibi supported by white witnesses, including his alleged victim. It didn't matter. As Ida B. Wells reported, "The verdict of the mob was that 'the crime had been committed and somebody had to hang for it, and if he, Peterson, was not guilty of [rape] he was guilty of some other crime.'"[18] Peterson was hanged, and then his dead body was shot repeatedly.

A total of 714 lynchings occurred during Roosevelt's presidency.[19] During the Taft presidency and the first Wilson administration, particularly from 1911 to 1917, the average yearly number of documented lynchings in America decreased. But in the aftermath of World War I, with segregationist President Woodrow Wilson serving a second term, they spiked up once again, to more than sixty a year from 1918 to 1922.[20]

Even after World War I many lynchings remained public events. They were promoted by local newspapers and well attended by all age groups. And neither state officials, local police, nor the federal government intervened to stop them.

Take, for example, the lynching that occurred on June 26, 1919, in Ellisville, Mississippi. The *Daily News* of Jackson, Mississippi, promoted it like a sporting event on its front page: "John Hartfield Will Be Lynched by Ellisville Mob at 5 O'Clock This Afternoon." The story continued, "Governor Bilbo says he is powerless to prevent it—Thousands of people are flocking into Ellisville to attend the event—Sheriff and Authorities are powerless to prevent it."[21] The governor and his minions were not powerless to stop the lynching of John Hartfield. They were complicit.

The first federal anti-lynching bill was introduced

in the House of Representatives in 1900. It was buried in committee. In 1922, the House of Representatives finally passed a federal anti-lynching bill.[22] The
bill was killed in the Senate by a southern filibuster.
From 1918 to 1948, federal legislation criminalizing
lynching was introduced in Congress nearly every
year.

Two anti-lynching bills passed the House of Representatives, one in 1937 and another in 1940. But, as
had happened in 1922, powerful southern Democrats
who controlled key Senate committees filibustered
both bills to death. Southern senators simply would
not allow a federal anti-lynching bill—legislation per-
ceived as a public insult to the South—to become law.

In 1937, 28% of Americans said Congress should
not pass a law making lynching a federal crime. In
the South, 43% opposed a federal lynching law.[23]

More than 200 federal anti-lynching bills were
introduced in Congress from 1900 to 2017. Not one
became law. Southern filibusters in the Senate, constitutional claims of states' rights and policing power,
intransigent racism, and white indifference to the
plight of black Americans scuttled justice each and
every time.

In 2018, 136 years after Ida B. Wells began her
work documenting lynching, the Senate finally passed
the Justice for Victims of Lynching Act.[24] The Senate

voted on the bill on December 19, 2018, with Mississippi senator Cindy Hyde-Smith presiding over the vote. A month earlier, Hyde-Smith had been caught on tape "joking that she would attend a 'public hanging' if invited by a supporter."[25]

There was no filibuster by southern senators this time. The Justice for Victims of Lynching Act passed the Senate unanimously and moved on to the House of Representatives. That is where the bill died—ignored by the Republican majority as the 115th Congress came to a close.

CODA

The United States of "Lyncherdom," as Mark Twain called America in his infamous essay, still does not have a law that makes lynching a federal crime (as of June 2020).

America's inability to confront its history of lynching and declare justice for its victims demonstrates the depth of racial animus that continues to animate our politics—racism that flows beneath the surface of society until it is summoned by those who willingly use fear and hate to build and maintain power.

Our failure to admit and take responsibility for past transgressions, to reconcile the past with the present, stands squarely between America and America's future. It is America's Achilles' heel, a vulnerability that demagogues have exploited for their own gain and our continued loss; and an open wound that cost George Floyd, and so many who went before him, their life and liberty.

The promise of *e pluribus unum* is a pipe dream in a society riven by racism.

LESSON 7

THE DRIVING OUT

CHINESE PERSECUTION, EXCLUSION, AND MASSACRE

I do not believe it to be just or the duty of Congress of the United States to make itself a pack of hounds to hunt down any race born and permitted to love on God's earth [applause].

They [the proponents of the Chinese Exclusion Act] ask us now to assail a race of human beings in large part of high civilization and high cultivation, to separate them from all other races of men on the face of the earth, to exclude them from American soil, to banish those who are now here from our midst, and to introduce a spirit of persecution, of race persecution into the legislation of Congress, whose glory has been in the past to make America an asylum of the oppressed of all nations.

—Speech on the floor of the
U.S. House of Representatives by
Congressman John Kasson, April 17, 1882

On April 17, 1882, the U.S. House of Representatives passed the Chinese Exclusion Act, the first American law to use race as a criterion for restricting immigration. Ignoring Iowa congressman John Kasson's warning that a vote for the bill sanctioned persecution, violated core American values, and transformed Congress into a pack of race-hunting "hounds," the House approved the act overwhelmingly—with 202 voting yes and only 37 opposed. Eleven days later the Senate followed suit, voting 32–15, and on May 6, 1882, President Chester Arthur signed the bill into law. Newspapers across the West applauded the federal government's action, with the *Dillon Tribune* in Montana writing, "The President on Monday last signed the Chinese Bill, now the heathen must go."[1]

32% of Americans agree immigration is eroding the traditional culture of the United States.[2]

Republicans and Democrats, abolitionists, former Know-Nothings and emergent nativists, organized labor, Progressives, and white supremacists all supported the Chinese Exclusion Act. Californians, in particular, demanded it.

In 1873, the *Los Angeles Herald* had warned of the Chinese "invasion of California." By 1879, hatred toward Chinese immigrants and Chinese Americans was etched into the California constitution.[3] The revised state constitution explicitly labeled Chinese as "dangerous to the well-being of the state" and denied them a path to citizenship even if they were native-born.

A national act excluding Chinese from America was the next logical step. During the debate on the Exclusion Act in the House and Senate, Congressman Albert Willis of Kentucky argued that Chinese immigration had "cursed" all "the Pacific States" and must be repulsed.[4] Senator Wilkinson Call of Florida intoned, "I believe as firmly as any in the superiority of the Caucasian race and the civilization which has come from it . . . the personal characteristics of the Chinese laborers, the personal characteristics of the Chinese who are brought here, are certainly very revolting, and are such as would naturally predispose, and properly predispose, any community against their admission in any number among them."[5] Senator George H. Pendleton of Ohio warned:

> We cannot bring in upon our civilization on the Pacific coast the hordes of Chinese devoted to everything which is repugnant to our religion, to our morals, to our habit, to our civilization, and expect it to increase in purity and power there. . . . [O]ur American nation, our American civilization [must] lead . . . by purifying, preserving, maintaining, consecrating the virtues we have thus far attained, let us not endanger them by association with vice and corruption, which can only contaminate and destroy.[6]

As Kasson cautioned in the quote that opened this lesson, the Chinese racial ban that became law in

1882 was not the end of the persecution of Chinese in America; it was just the beginning. Congress's targeted ban validated the othering trope advanced in major newspapers for years that the Chinese were a dangerous, inferior horde—an invading race of diseased Mongolian lepers—and encouraged public vigilantism.

28% of Americans today agree strongly that children born in America whose parents are illegal immigrants should not automatically receive U.S. citizenship.[7]

From 1849 through 1906, there were more than 200 so-called roundups of Chinese Americans in California alone.[8] After 1882, the violence increased and spread. From 1883 to 1885, white mobs rioted in more than a hundred cities and towns across the West to drive Chinese populations away. Across the Washington Territory, Oregon, California, Wyoming Territory, Colorado, and Nevada, Chinese-owned stores were looted, property was stolen, and homes were burned. In the growing mayhem of what would become known as the "driving out," many Chinese and Chinese Americans lost not only their livelihoods but also their lives.[9]

On September 2, 1885, in Rock Springs, Wyoming Territory, the violence reached an apex when at least twenty-eight people of Chinese descent were murdered and many more injured by a rioting mob of more than 150 white miners. The riot started with an altercation that left one miner dead, a pickax in his skull. It grew into a white wilding that rampaged across the town. Surveying the aftermath of the Rock Springs Massacre two days later, the *New York Times* reported, "Many of the bullets fired at the fleeing Chinamen found their mark. Lying in the smoldering embers where Chinatown [had] stood were found ten charred and shapeless trunks [bodies], sending up a noisome stench, while another, which had evidently been dragged from the ashes by boys, was found in the sagebrush nearby."[10]

After the riot had run its course and the Chinese had fled Rock Springs, sixteen whites were arrested for a list of crimes that included robbery, murder, and arson. All of them were acquitted. Not a single witness to the massacre stepped forward to testify. To add insult to injury, hundreds of whites happily gathered in Cheyenne to celebrate the acquittal and release of the rioting robbers, murderers, and arsonists.[11] The lesson of Rock Springs was clear: the Chinese other would not be protected by local government authorities or the law. This was as true in territorial mining towns like Rock Springs as it was in growing cities like Tacoma, where the city's mayor led the purge of Chinese and the burning of Chinatown two months later.[12]

The Chinese Exclusion Act was replaced in 1892 by the Geary Act, which extended the exclusion of Chinese for an additional ten years, maintained the ban on citizenship, and added a new odious restriction—what people of Chinese descent living in America dubbed the Dog Tag Law. This provision forced all Chinese to obtain a government-issued identity card (a certificate of residence) within a year and carry the card with them at all times. Those who did not comply could be sentenced to one year of hard labor or immediate deportation.

29% of Americans agree that all Muslims, including those who are U.S. citizens, should be required to carry a government-issued identification card with them at all times that would have to be shown to state and local police officers on request.[13]

From due process to equal protection concerns, the Dog Tag Law raised numerous constitutional questions. Those questions were tested in federal court, and the white supremacists prevailed. In *Fong Yue Ting v. United States* (1893), the Supreme Court affirmed the government's right to deport Chinese immigrants, including those who had lived in the country for years. For the first time, deportation became a legally recognized tool of immigration enforcement, setting the outlines of the debate that would occur more than a century later around the Deferred Action for Childhood Arrivals (DACA) program and the status of young undocumented immigrants, known as "Dreamers" (from a 2001 law, the Development, Relief, and Education for Alien Minors [DREAM] Act).

Congress made the exclusion of Chinese laborers from the United States permanent in 1902. This remained the situation until 1943, when World War II made improving relations with China a matter of national security. In that year, the Chinese Exclusion Act of 1882 and its successors were repealed by Congress and replaced by a quota system. But racial animus toward Chinese was not extinguished; instead, it was reimagined. From a country of over 500 million, a total of 105 Chinese would be allowed to immigrate to the United States each year.

CODA

One year after the Chinese Exclusion Act became law, closing the nation to Chinese immigrants whose labor had helped build America's intercontinental railroads, Emma Lazarus wrote "The New Colossus," the sonnet so many Americans know and cherish. Boldly affirming the exceptional, aspirational tradition of America, Lazarus declared, "Give me your tired, your poor, / Your huddled masses yearning to breathe free, / The wretched refuse of your teeming shore. / Send these, the homeless, tempest-tost to me, / I lift my lamp beside the golden door."

A year after the lives of at least twenty-eight Chinese and Chinese Americans were taken in Rock Springs, Wyoming Territory, the Statue of Liberty with her lamp lighting the way to freedom and opportunity for all was dedicated on Ellis Island. And the year after the racial and class-based exclusion of Chinese immigrants was made a permanent part of U.S. law, Emma Lazarus's transcendent illumination of American values was cast in bronze and affixed to the pedestal on which Lady Liberty stands.

This history lays bare the two competing impulses in American history: the competition between aspirational Enlightenment-inspired equality and authoritarianism bathed in white supremacy. A part of Lazarus's sonnet says, "'Keep, ancient lands, your storied pomp!' cries she / With silent lips." Ancient hatreds steeped in race and class beset those ancient lands—hatreds that infused the worldviews of the proponents of Chinese exclusion and which they were unafraid to declare.

These ancient hatreds are not dead. Racial othering lives on today, quite unabashedly, in our society and our government. And those who use it are hard at work trying to appropriate and rewrite parts of American history to refashion the past and make it more conducive to achieving their goals today.

To see how our history is being spun to justify the unjustifiable, look no further than the recent statements of Ken Cuccinelli, the acting head of U.S. Citizenship and Immigration Services, on immigration policy. First, Cuccinelli deployed a bastardized version of Lazarus's "The New Colossus" to defend the Trump administration's new, more restrictive immigration policy, saying, "Give me your tired and your poor *who can stand on their own two feet and who will not become a public charge.*" Then, dancing with Senate white supremacists like Call and Pendleton from the 1880s, Cuccinelli claimed that Lazarus's sonnet referred only to white "people coming from Europe."[14]

As Cuccinelli knows or should know, "The New Colossus" was written as a pointed rebuke of white supremacism, and it remains so today. While American authoritarians like Cuccinelli may try to appropriate and spin its meaning to advance their exclusionary views, the history of "The New Colossus" is clear: Lady Liberty welcomes all equally.

When the votes on the Chinese Exclusion Act of 1882 were counted in the U.S. House of Representatives, Congressman John Kasson, whose passionate defense of America's aspirational tradition framed the beginning of this chapter, voted in favor of the exclusion of Chinese from America. Kasson justified the abandonment of his principles with this dissembling statement:

> I wish it to be distinctly understood that this side of the House in sustaining this bill [voting for the Chinese Exclusion Act of 1882], only does so for the sake of a just trial of the question whether there is in it a relief from the danger to our institution, to our system of labor, and to our system of society on the Pacific coast. If this bill went one hair's breadth beyond the principles which I have referred to and should provoke antipathy and war of races, I should hold it to be the duty of this Congress to reject it. We, on this side of the House, have been and will remain the party of liberty, of justice, and of hospitality to all the oppressed

nationalities of the earth; and may the day be far distant when we shall abandon that crowning glory of our history.

The lesson here is as clear today as it was nearly 140 years ago: if you want America to live up to its promise, watch what those in power do, not what they say.

LESSON 8

FEAR AS A PATH TO POWER
THE PALMER RAIDS

> Woe be it to the man that seeks to stand in our way in this day of high resolution when every principle we hold dearest is to be vindicated and made secure.
> —President Woodrow Wilson[1]

The first Palmer Raids, led by the U.S. Department of Justice and fueled by the growing fear of communists, anarchists, and radicals sweeping America, took place on November 7, 1919. Mitchel Lavrowsky, a teacher at the People's House in Manhattan, described what happened:

At about 8:00 o'clock in the evening, while I was teaching algebra and Russian, an agent of the Department of Justice opened the door of the school, walked in with a revolver in his hands and ordered everybody in the school to step aside, then [he] ordered me to step towards him. I wear eye-glasses and the agent of the Department of Justice ordered me to take them off. Then without any provocation,

[he] struck me on the head and simultaneously two others struck and beat me brutally.[2]

Lavrowsky was fifty years old at the time of the raid. He had emigrated from Odessa, Russia, where he had been a high school principal. He was married, had two children, and hoped to become a citizen of the United States.

38% of Americans say immigrants are a threat to public safety.[3]

Within minutes of barging into his classroom, federal agents had beaten Lavrowsky so brutally he could not stand. But he wasn't taken to a hospital. With hundreds of others, he was taken in for questioning. The beating was not an anomaly. Department agents (maybe it is more accurate to describe them as thugs) raged through the People's House:

They broke up and destroyed most of the furniture in the place, including desks and typewriting machines. They "beat up" the persons in the place, amounting to several hundreds, with black-jacks and stair rails. . . . [They] herded the students to the stairways, beating them as they went, shoving them from the landing on to the stairway so that many fell and rolled down the stairs and were trampled by those who were shoved after them.

In all, "several hundred prisoners were taken to the office of the Department of Justice at 13 Park Row and there put through the third degree of inquisition."[4]

Most of the people assaulted and dragged in for questioning were rounded up illegally—there were just a few arrest warrants issued before the raid began. More than 80 percent of the hundreds hauled to 13 Park Row were quickly released after they were questioned and found to be "innocent of any wrongdoing."[5]

They were the lucky ones. Ninety-seven men, some of whom were arrested in a different raid in Connecticut, and others who made the mistake of trying to see their friends who had been dragged away to the Hartford jail, were held for five months in "practically solitary confinement." Locked away, some were "beaten or threatened with hanging or suffocation" during repeated questioning by Department of Justice agents.[6]

The November raids in New York City, Hartford, Philadelphia, Chicago, and other cities were ordered by A. Mitchell Palmer, the attorney general of the United States.[7] They were carried out by Department of Justice agents working with local police and, in some cases, volunteer vigilantes. While extensive in scope, the raids were simply a dress rehearsal for the mayhem Palmer and J. Edgar Hoover, his newly appointed head of the General Intelligence Division of the Bureau of Investigation, planned to launch across the United States in the coming months.

To the press, Palmer declared the November raids a success, claiming that ammunition, arms, bomb-making equipment, and subversive literature had been found and that the hundreds arrested would be deported.[8] He also announced that in Chicago he had uncovered communist "plans for a 'reign of terror'" in the city.[9]

Palmer's claims were false, but the news media ate them up and clamored for more. Forget about the flagrant violations of constitutional niceties like warrants, due process, and freedom of speech and affiliation by the Department of Justice. As the *Washington Post* declared in an editorial: "There is no time to waste on hairsplitting over infringement of liberties."[10]

President Wilson had appointed Alexander Mitchell Palmer attorney general in March 1919—four months after the armistice was signed with Germany and World War I hostilities ended. Palmer succeeded progressive Democrat Thomas Gregory, who, working with the head of the Bureau of Investigation and the U.S. postmaster general, had already implemented a sweeping effort to stifle dissent, stop protests, and jail those identified as radicals. (Yes, political progressives can act like fascists, too.) Wilson asked Gregory to step down after a massive raid he led to round up draft dodgers in New York City detained 75,000 citizens for three days and created a public relations nightmare.[11]

Palmer was a Quaker pacifist with an enviable list of progressive credentials. In his six years in Congress, he was a civil libertarian who supported child labor laws, a graduated income tax, and women's rights. He was also an ambitious politician who had set his sights on the White House and was looking for a platform to raise his national visibility.

While the war in Europe was over, Palmer took office as attorney general in a time of growing civil unrest in the United States. Strikes, rising unemployment and inflation, race riots, and fears of Bolshevism rattled America. The turbulence was not imaginary. In the weeks after Palmer was appointed, nationwide mail bombings began. Thirty-six bombs, set to explode on May Day 1919, were sent to members of the Senate and Supreme Court, other government officials, and leading bankers and businessmen. On June 2, 1919, more bombs were detonated, including one targeting the new attorney general. Carlo Valdinoci, an Italian anarchist, hand-delivered that bomb in a briefcase to the front door of Palmer's house at 2132 R Street in Washington. The device went off prematurely, however, killing Valdinoci, blowing out windows throughout the neighborhood, and destroying the front of Palmer's house.

Reports of the bombings headlined newspapers across the country, and Palmer vowed to bring the perpetrators and their associates to justice. An essay by Palmer, "The Case Against the 'Reds,'" published months after the bombings, reveals his state of mind at the time and his political calculation that standing for law and order and against anarchists, radicals, and Reds was a sure path to power. Palmer wrote:

Like a prairie-fire, the blaze of revolution was sweeping over every American institution of law and order a year ago. It was eating its way into the homes of the American workman, its sharp tongues of revolutionary heat were licking the altars of the churches, leaping into the belfry of the school bell, crawling into the sacred corners of American homes . . . , burning up the foundations of society. . . . The Department of Justice will pursue the attack of these "Reds" upon the Government of the United States with vigilance, and no alien, advocating the overthrow of existing law and order in this country, shall escape arrest and prompt deportation.[12]

Step one was to identify the enemy in our midst. Palmer turned to Congress for money to do so, established a new department—the General Intelligence Division (GID), aka the Radical Division—in the Bureau of Investigation, and by August had hired the twenty-four-year-old J. Edgar Hoover to run it. Hoover wasted little time assembling a list of over 60,000 suspected radicals, agitators, and anarchists and built the GID into "the storm center of the anti-radical hysteria" sweeping the country.[13]

With Hoover's enemies list assembled, step two was imperative: the launching of raids across the United States simultaneously so that anti-American radicals would not melt away and escape the government dragnet. With their tactics road-tested in November, Palmer and Hoover planned a sweeping nationwide raid for the day after New Year's 1920.

On January 2, 1920, the Department of Justice launched raids in more than thirty cities across the United States. Arrest estimates vary between 3,000 and 10,000 people. Like the test raids in November, most arrests were warrantless and indiscriminate, with many people thrown in jail for merely being in the wrong place at the wrong time or having a foreign accent. Jails in cities like Newark and Jersey City were overflowing with arrested suspects.[14]

The sweeping and lawless prosecution of the raids and their aftermath were succinctly captured by a reporter writing for *The Nation*:

> On January 2 Arthur L. Barkey, chief agent of the Department of Justice in Detroit, received an order from Attorney General Palmer instructing Mr. Barkey, according to his own statement, to raid the headquarters of . . . the Communist party . . . in a "supreme effort to break the back of radicalism" in Detroit. As a result, eight hundred men were imprisoned for from three-to-six days in a dark, windowless, narrow corridor running around the big central areaway of the city's antiquated Federal Buildings. . . . What was the crime of the eight hundred? The crime was that these men were attending a dance or studying physical geography and other sciences in a hall known as the House of the Masses, the headquarters of the Communist Party in Detroit.[15]

A full three months after the raid in Detroit, 150 of those arrested continued to languish in jail. Many had not been charged with a crime, and none knew when or how they would be released.[16] Commenting on the Palmer raids, George Anderson, a judge appointed by President Wilson to the federal Court of Appeals for the First Circuit, said, "More lawless proceedings are hard to conceive."[17]

With the press and many in the Washington political establishment solidly in his corner, Palmer took full credit for directing the January dragnet. He then turned to stoking public fear again by warning that Hoover's GID had now identified more than 300,000 dangerous communists who were still at large in America. Two months later, on March 1, 1920, cashing in on the press and public attention, Palmer launched a "law and order" campaign for president. He was the first Democrat to throw his hat in the ring.

Palmer's candidacy fueled mounting criticism of his raids and his attacks on organized labor. Seeing shadows, doubling down on the politics of fear, or both, Palmer announced in late April that Department of Justice agents had uncovered a Red revolution and "death plot" to murder "more than a score of federal and state officials." The attacks were scheduled for May 1, 1920—a year to the day after the first wave of mail bombings. According to Palmer, "The [planned] assassinations and assaults . . . , were included in the May Day program organized by the communist labor party and other radical elements and were in addition to strikes and other disturbances."[18]

When May Day came and went without bombings, mass demonstrations, or any revolutionary disturbances, Palmer's credibility was shredded. Writing with acid instead of ink, the *New York Tribune* noted, "The Red revolution scheduled to come to America yesterday must have missed the boat."[19] In New York City, the eleven thousand police, Secret Service agents, and patriotic volunteers ready to defend New York were left with little to do. Only one man was arrested with a Red handbill in his hand.

Palmer's use of fear to pave his path to power had reached a limit. While the Red fever that swept the country was still hot, Palmer's reputation was in tatters. The fear that had enabled him to ignore federal law and abridge fundamental constitutional protections no longer insulated him from criticism. The dam broke quickly.

On May 28, 1920, twelve lawyers, including future Supreme Court justice Felix Frankfurter, wrote and signed a "Report to the American People upon the Illegal Practices of the United States Department of Justice." Published under the auspices of the National Popular Government League—the forerunner of the American Civil Liberties Union—the eighty-plus-page document reads like a criminal indictment of Palmer and the Department of Justice. It begins as follows:

> For more than six months we, the undersigned lawyers, whose sworn duty it is to uphold the Constitution and Laws of the United States, have seen with growing apprehension the continued violation of that Constitution and breaking of those Laws

by the Department of Justice of the United States
government.... We are concerned solely with
bringing to the attention of the American people
the utterly illegal acts which have been committed
by those charged with the highest duty of enforcing the laws—acts which have caused widespread
suffering and unrest, have struck at the foundation
of American free institutions, and have brought the
name of our country into disrepute.[20]

The report then lays out a stunning bill of particulars: Cruel punishments unthinkable in America
had become usual. Hundreds of citizens and aliens
had been arrested without warrants and imprisoned
indefinitely. Department of Justice agents had broken
into homes and offices without warrants, and destroyed and seized property. Undercover agents had
instigated acts that may be criminal. Witnesses had
been forced and intimidated by Department of Justice
agents to bear witness against themselves. And the attorney general had used propaganda against radicals
in a deliberate misuse of his office.

In short, the Department of Justice had gone
rogue, regularly violating constitutional guarantees it
was charged with protecting. The attorney general, A.
Mitchell Palmer, had broken his oath of office, and
his renegade Radical Division was acting more like
state security forces in Russia than a law-abiding department of the United States government.

The next month, at the Democratic Convention
in San Francisco, Palmer conceded defeat on the

thirty-eighth ballot. He remained attorney general for another nine months. During that time, Congress, which had supported Palmer's raids or, at least, not impeded them, investigated him.

CODA

While it is easy to blame Palmer for his instrumental, unconstitutional actions, there are two deeper lessons in this story. First, as Palmer's biographer aptly notes, "If Palmer was one of the most dangerous men in our history, it was not because he attempted to impose his rule or his policies upon the people, but because he tried to win power by carefully attuning himself to what he felt were the strong desires of most Americans."[21]

Palmer fed those desires, but he didn't start them. President Wilson and others also bear responsibility for inflaming the violent passions of the American public and allowing self-interested men like Palmer and Hoover to shred the Constitution.

35% of Americans think there is a great deal or fair amount of extremism among American Muslims.[22]

Second, while Palmer retired from public service at the end of Wilson's presidency in 1921, his young henchman in the Department of Justice carried on. Three years later, in 1924, J. Edgar Hoover was named the director of the Bureau of Investigation.

When the Federal Bureau of Investigation was established in 1935, he became its first director and served in that post for thirty-seven years, where he continued to perfect many of the unconstitutional tactics he had employed during the Palmer raids.

The lesson here is clear: When institutions like the Department of Justice ignore the Constitution and flaunt the rule of law, changing leadership at the top is not a sufficient remedy. The institution itself must be changed to protect democracy. A complete housecleaning was needed. Hoover and those who aided and abetted his work during the raids should have been shown the door, and a law-abiding culture instituted within the department whose job it is to follow and enforce the rule of law.

LESSON 9

GALVANIZING GROUP IDENTITY
A NAZI DEMONSTRATION
OF TRUE AMERICANISM

The speaker on the podium in the center of the massive stage was Gerhard Wilhelm Kunze, the national propaganda director of the German American Bund. The date was February 20, 1939. Held in Madison Square Garden in New York City, the event was billed as a "pro-American rally." Posters scattered throughout the city (preserved today in the archives of the U.S. Holocaust Memorial Museum) promoted the affair as a "mass demonstration for true Americanism."

In 1938, 54% of Americans agreed that "the persecution of Jews in Europe has been partly their own fault." Another 11% thought the persecution of Jews was "entirely their own fault." [1]

Styled as an American Reichsparteitag (the annual mass gathering of the Nazi Party held in Nuremberg by Hitler between 1923 and 1938, intended to stoke fascist fervor and galvanize Nazi identity), the rally celebrated white supremacy, anti-Semitism, and the nation's first president, George Washington (Bund members claimed that Washington was America's first fascist).

Directly behind Kunze stood a thirty-foot-tall portrait of a proud George Washington bracketed by American flags and Nazi swastikas. The stage itself was packed with members of the Ordnungsdienst, a vigilante paramilitary force whose uniforms were knock-offs of those worn by the Waffen SS. American Bund youth—some of whom attended Nazi summer camps held each year across America in places like Andover, New Jersey; Grafton, Wisconsin; and La Crescenta, California—were also onstage, joined by a line of drummers whose martial beat had set the pace for the parade that kicked off the event.

Speaking from the raised dais, Kunze spun the German American Bund's authoritarian account of American history, claiming that "the spirit which opened the West and built our country is the spirit of the militant white man. . . . It has then always been very much American to protect the Aryan character of this nation."

Kunze and the other leaders of the German American Bund spoke to 22,000 Americans in the Garden that night. An estimated 100,000 Americans surrounded the hall in protest. Protected by 1,700 members of the New York Police Department, however, the Nazi rally continued unimpeded for hours.

You may be wondering whether some of the people

celebrating the Reichsparteitag at Madison Square Garden on the cold night of February 20, 1939, were good people (using the standard set by Donald Trump for the 2017 Charlottesville "Unite the Right" white supremacist rally). The honest answer is no. Like their white nationalist, anti-Semitic kin who marched in Charlottesville, Virginia, seventy-eight years later, the Nazi followers gathered in Madison Square Garden placed the superiority of their chosen identity before their humanity. Both demonstrations were geared to galvanize group identification, showcase group power, and expunge any lingering doubts about their self-professed superiority.

The hateful message encoded in both mass rallies was clear: *Aryans are supreme. They are superior. They are the true Americans. Do not tread on us. Join us or fear us.*

Like the woman in Charlottesville who lost her life as she protested the 2017 gathering, there was a heroic American at Madison Square Garden in 1939 who dared to challenge this hate rally. His name was Isadore Greenbaum. And he was kicked, beaten, and bloodied by the vigilante Ordnungsdienst for daring to stand up to the hate flowing freely at the Garden that night.

Greenbaum, a twenty-six-year-old plumber from Brooklyn, saw the Nazi symbols hanging around Madison Square, the "Stop Jewish Domination of Christian Americans" posters, and the placards urging "Wake Up America. Smash Jewish Communism."

From news reports of the Night of the Long Knives in 1934, the Austrian Anschluss in early 1938, and Kristallnacht later in 1938, Isadore must have known something about how Nazis brutally dealt with any opposition.[2] And he may even have known of the six concentration camps Hitler had already built across Germany.

Greenbaum watched the crowd stretch out their arms and raise their hands in a Nazi salute to both the American and Nazi flags. (There is some disagreement whether the crowd was using the Nazi salute or the Bellamy salute. The Bellamy salute is a palm-out gesture that the author of the Pledge of Allegiance, Francis Bellamy, thought should be used when saying the pledge. The difference between the salutes is very hard to discern, demonstrating how easy it was for the German American Bund to blur the lines between American patriotism and obeisance to Nazism and the Fuhrer.) He listened to the Pledge of Allegiance read from a podium festooned with swastikas and intoned by a crowd who saw no contradiction between the call for liberty and justice for all in the pledge, and the Aryan exceptionalism and exclusionism celebrated that night. He listened to Fritz Julius Kuhn, America's Bundesführer, rally the crowd with a rousing speech. Kuhn, who called President Franklin Delano Roosevelt "Franklin Rosenfield" and the New Deal the "Jew Deal," seamlessly adopted the fascists' playbook. He attacked the press, labeling it a lapdog of the Jewish conspiracy threatening the United States.

"Ladies and gentlemen, fellow Americans, American patriots," Kuhn began. "I am sure I do not come before you tonight as a complete stranger. You all have heard of me through the Jewish-controlled press as a creature with horns, a cloven hoof, and a long tail."

The audience loved it.

He went on: "We, with American ideals, demand that our government should be returned to the American people who founded it." Then Kuhn, like any true-believing fascist, turned to attack the unworthy others who were trying to wrest America from its Aryan destiny: "If you ask what we are actively fighting for under our charter, first, a socially just white, Gentile-ruled United States. Second, Gentile-controlled labor unions, free from Jewish Moscow-directed domination."

The historical footage of Kuhn's speech is a dystopian nightmare—a foul mashup of newsreels populated by ordinary-looking American extras incongruously sporting Nazi armbands. Finally, Greenbaum acted. Jumping onstage, Greenbaum pulled the cords attached to Kuhn's microphone, knocking it over, and yelled, "Down with Hitler." He was immediately swarmed and tackled by the vigilante Ordnungsdienst on the stage as a security force. Kicked and punched repeatedly and stripped of his pants, to the cheers of the American fascists witnessing the pummeling, Greenbaum suffered a broken nose, black eye, and welts across his body before the police intervened and dragged him from the stage.

CODA

Greenbaum was arrested and fined $25. His crime? Civil disobedience. But he had no regrets. Resisting American Nazism was worth the price.

A few years later, Greenbaum enlisted in the navy and went off to fight the Nazis in World War II. His act of defiance—one Jew surrounded by 22,000 American Nazis energized and unified by the hate and vitriol they had heard during hours of speeches—is an example of true courage, the courage sometimes required to stand up for American values when others willingly forsake them.

Resisting would-be autocrats from the left, right, or center and questioning their allegiance to the Constitution and the rule of law is the duty of each and every American no matter their party or ideology.

LESSON 10

SILENCE OF THE LAW

THE INTERNMENT OF
AMERICAN JAPANESE AND THE
UGLY ABYSS OF RACISM

21% of Americans still approve of the executive order issued by Franklin Roosevelt in 1942 that forcibly relocated Americans of Japanese descent and their families to internment camps during World War II.

—YouGov national survey,
January 15–19, 2016
Economist/YouGov Poll[1]

George Takei, the actor of *Star Trek* fame who is now a well-known author, activist, and social influencer, was five years old when the soldiers came to his home to take him and his family away. Decades later, during an interview on *PBS NewsHour*, he described what happened:

We were at the front window just gazing out, and, suddenly, we saw two soldiers marching up the driveway, carrying rifles with shiny bayonets. They stomped up the front porch, and with their fists, began pounding on the door. And that, I can't forget.[2]

The Takei family did not live in some faraway, lawless land ruled by an autocrat and hostile to due process and civil rights. The Takeis lived in Los Angeles, California. They were caught up in the exclusion, roundup, and internment of American citizens of Japanese descent that began in the western United States a few months after the Japanese attack on Pearl Harbor.

> My father came out, answered the door. And we were ordered to leave the house. They were questioning my mother. And when she came out, she had our baby sister in one arm and a huge duffel bag in the other. Tears were streaming down her face. That was, to us, shocking and absolutely scary.[3]

The duffel bag carried by George's mother contained most of the earthly possessions the Takeis would be allowed to take with them that day.[4] Like so many Japanese Americans sent to internment camps, the rest of their belongings were left behind—looted and lost.

For almost four years, the family was held in remote camps in Arkansas and, later, Northern California. The compounds were ringed with barbed wire. But "at least during the internment, when I was just five years old," George Takei wrote in 2018, "I was not taken from my parents."[5] Separating children from parents was too cruel and inhumane a step for America circa 1940. Today, it is just one of a growing list of federal policies that are reshaping what America is and how Americans are viewed in the world.

What brought fully armed soldiers to the doors of Japanese Americans in 1942? Fear, racism, and the abrogation of human rights and the rule of law that so often ensues when war is in the air. As the Roman philosopher and statesman Marcus Tullius Cicero warned almost a hundred years before the birth of Christ, "Inter arma enim silent leges"—in times of war, the law is silent.

* * *

The Imperial Japanese Navy Air Service attacked Pearl Harbor on December 7, 1941. The strike devastated the United States Pacific Fleet, sinking four battleships, damaging four more, and in the mayhem killing more than 2,400 Americans. It was a day "which will live in infamy," declared President Roosevelt to a joint session of Congress twenty-four hours later. America and Japan were now at war.

In the hours after the attack, the FBI, under the direction of J. Edgar Hoover, began detaining Japanese immigrants and aliens on its Custodial Detention list (CDL). The list was the product of domestic surveillance of organizations and individuals initiated by Hoover in 1939. An urgent FBI telegram to its field offices ordered that anyone on the list who was rated A, B, or C (A's were considered the most dangerous threat) was to be taken into custody immediately.

By December 8, 736 Japanese immigrants in the continental United States had been detained. By February 1942, the total number of Japanese immigrants and Americans of Japanese descent taken and imprisoned by the FBI grew to 2,192.[6]

While the FBI moved quickly, the scope of its arrests was limited. Francis Biddle, the attorney general of the United States, ordered the FBI to exercise restraint in hopes of avoiding the "mass internment and the persecution of aliens that had characterized the First World War."[7] Biddle was not alone. Politicians of all stripes initially spoke up in support of protecting the rights of Americans of Japanese descent.

Governor Culbert Olson of California, the state that had the largest Japanese American population and was considered the next target of the Imperial Japanese Navy Air Service, captured the political zeitgeist in the days after Pearl Harbor by saying, "The vast majority of American-born and foreign-born Japanese in California are loyal to the United States and anxious to serve its interests."[8] Others, like Washington congressman John Coffee, preached reason and the rule of law: "Let us not make a mockery of our Bill of Rights by mistreating these folks."[9]

By the end of 1941, the head of the Western Defense Command, General John DeWitt, concluded that there was no longer a risk of a Japanese invasion of the West Coast.[10] In early 1942 the Office of Naval Intelligence estimated that only 3 percent of Americans of Japanese descent were possible threats and that most of them had already been detained by the FBI.[11] But while the military threat to the American mainland lessened, public fears about Japanese Americans grew.

Rumors of Japanese spies and saboteurs in California and other West Coast states spread. Media fearmongering fanned the conspiratorial flames. Influential journalists like Walter Lippmann fed them, warning that "the Pacific Coast is in imminent danger of a combined attack from within and without."[12] The absence of an attack so far was, to Lippmann, "a sign that the blow [that will come] is well organized; that it is held back until it can be struck with maximum effect."[13]

Politicians like Earl Warren, the attorney general of California who would later become the chief justice of the United States, jumped on the conspiracy bandwagon. At a congressional hearing held in San Francisco, he testified that some Japanese Americans had appeared to purchase farms in strategic locations to maximize their ability to aid the Imperial Navy's invasion when the time came.[14] Interest groups on the right, on the left, and in the center called for the detainment of Americans of Japanese descent. Even the American Civil Liberties Union split into pro and con factions over the internment issue. Whipped into a fever, public opinion reached a hysterical tipping point with a politically expedient solution: lock them up.

On February 11, Secretary of War Henry Stimson presented President Franklin Roosevelt with four options for dealing with American citizens of Japanese descent. In a three-minute phone conversation on the matter, Roosevelt instructed Stimson to make the decision and "be as reasonable as you can."[15] A week later, Roosevelt issued Executive Order 9066, empowering the military to establish areas from which "any or all persons may be excluded," and put Stimson's War Department in charge of the effort.[16]

Roosevelt's order did not mention Japanese Americans. That dirty work was left to the Department of War. Penalties for not complying with an exclusion order were also absent from Roosevelt's directive. That dirty work was left to Congress, which with Public Law 503 made it a crime punishable by imprisonment for anyone, including American citizens, to disobey the order. The resulting expulsion and detainment policy was a tour de force of "political buck-passing . . . designed so that no single legal pronouncement explicitly ordered relocation and internment on racial grounds. The Roosevelt administration and the Army expected legal challenges, and they wanted to win them."[17]

The Justice Department's policy of following the law and protecting the civil rights of American citizens of Japanese descent was scrapped. Attorney General Biddle and the voices of moderation and constitutional due process had lost to the furies of fear. Japanese Americans were no longer treated as individuals who were innocent until proven guilty. Instead, they were judged as a group who was presumed guilty, without right of appeal, simply because of their ancestry.[18]

General DeWitt was put in charge of implementing the policy. A few weeks after Pearl Harbor, DeWitt had questioned the legality of internment, saying, "An American citizen, after all, is an American citizen."[19] Once Executive Order 9066 was issued, he put his doubts aside: "A Jap is a Jap, and it makes no difference if he is an American citizen."[20] With the constitutional niceties of due process and civil rights kicked to the curb by the commander in chief, restraint no longer appeared necessary to DeWitt and many other Americans.

In 1942, 48% of Americans said Japanese Americans who were in internment camps should not be allowed to return to their homes on the Pacific coast when the war was over.

When these 48% were asked what should be done with the Japanese Americans in the internment camps, 63% said send them back to Japan or put them out of this country, while 10% wanted them to remain imprisoned.[21]

In 1942, General DeWitt detained and sent to internment camps more than 119,000 Issei (first-generation immigrants from Japan) and Nisei (children of first-generation immigrants born in the United States). Approximately two-thirds of those imprisoned were birthright American citizens. They were distributed among ten different camps spread across

California, Idaho, Arizona, Arkansas, Utah, and Colorado.

"Camp" is a deceptive euphemism. The prisons were set in remote and desolate locations ringed with barbed wire. Internees were required to construct many of the buildings where they would live for the next several years. Newsreels from the time described the internees as "merely dislocated people." A more apt description of the Americans in their ranks is people disowned by their country and denied their constitutional rights.

In 1943, the War Relocation Authority administered a loyalty test to all internees seventeen years of age or older. Those who passed the test could leave the camps for work (if they could find it) or school (if they could gain admittance). Many also signed up to serve in the military of the country that had imprisoned them. By late 1944, the government began closing some of the camps (camp closings were intentionally delayed until after the presidential election held in November). The last camp was closed in March 1946. Almost 50,000 internees left the camps before they were closed.

During war, the powers of the president are at an apex, and the rule of law is too often abridged. The Supreme Court's silence on the internment of Issei and Nisei during World War II was indeed deafening. The Court's decision in 1944 in *Korematsu v. United States* upheld "the constitutionality of a policy of detaining U.S. citizens who had committed no crimes" except for belonging to an othered group.[22] The ugly reality of the Court's *Korematsu* decision was laid bare in Justice Frank Murphy's stinging dissent:

> This exclusion of "all persons of Japanese ancestry, both alien and non-alien," from the Pacific Coast area on a plea of military necessity in the absence of martial law ought not to be approved [by the Supreme Court]. Such exclusion goes over "the very brink of constitutional power" and falls into the ugly abyss of racism.

To this day, *Korematsu* is considered—along with *Dred Scott*—one of the worst opinions ever handed down by the high court.[23]

* * *

Three decades after the last internment camp closed, President Gerald Ford took the unusual step of declaring Roosevelt's Executive Order 9066 null and void. Seven years later, Judge Marilyn Patel of the Ninth Circuit Court vacated Fred Korematsu's conviction after finding that the government had suppressed important evidence in his case. The suppressed evidence revealed that in 1942 the government did not consider Japanese Americans a domestic military threat. Military necessity, the justification for exclusion and internment, was thus a sham. (Judge Patel's ruling on the facts did not affect the Supreme Court's decision on the constitutionality of the exclusion order.)

These details were unearthed by historian Peter

Irons and the Commission on Wartime Relocation and Internment of Civilians, established by Congress in 1980. Based in part on the commission's work, Congress passed the Civil Liberties Act of 1988, which apologized for the internment policy and paid reparations to survivors. President Ronald Reagan signed the Civil Liberties Act on August 10, 1988, during a moving ceremony in Washington attended by members of Congress and members of the Japanese American community, including Norman Mineta, an American of Japanese descent who spent three years in a camp when he was ten years old. Mineta later graduated from the University of California at Berkeley, served in military intelligence, and was elected mayor of San Jose. By 1988, he was serving his seventh term in the U.S. House of Representatives.

President Reagan began his speech at the ceremony by saying, "We gather here today to right a great wrong. . . ." After detailing the history of the internment of Japanese Americans, Reagan continued, "[H]ere we admit a wrong, here we reaffirm our commitment as a nation to equal justice under the law."[24] In his easygoing, approachable style, Reagan then went on to tell a story about another observance held more than four decades earlier, in 1945. At that event, General Joseph W. Stilwell presented a Distinguished Service Cross to Mary Masuda, who had just been released from internment. Her brother, who was the posthumous recipient of the medal, had died in battle protecting his unit from German troops while she was imprisoned.

One of the speakers at the 1945 event was a Hollywood star. The actor thanked the Masuda family for their sacrifice and said this: "Blood that has soaked into the sands of a beach is all of one color. America stands unique in the world: the only country not founded on race but on an ideal. Not in spite of, but because of our polyglot background, we have had all the strength in the world. That is the American way."[25]

The star who spoke those words at Masuda's ceremony at the end of World War II was Ronald Reagan. Closing the circle on August 10, 1988, Reagan concluded his remarks with the same refrain spoken decades before: "And yes, the ideal of liberty and justice for all—that is still the American way."

CODA

Four decades after the fact, America apologized to the Americans of Japanese descent for what their country did to them. But can we be certain that something like this will never happen again in America? Can we be certain that the ideal of liberty and justice for all is the *only* American way?

The truth is we cannot. The authoritarian impulse in America, the growing power of the presidency, and the failing public faith in our institutions and, as a result, their failing power make infringements on constitutional rights and the rule of law more probable, not less—especially in a time of national emergency.

Supreme Court justice Antonin Scalia recognized the clear and present peril that continually confronts America. Speaking in Hawaii a few years before his untimely death, Scalia, answering a question about the *Korematsu* decision, said:

> You are kidding yourself if you think the same thing will not happen again. "Inter arma enim silent leges" . . . In times of war, the laws fall silent. That's what was going on—the panic about the war and the invasion of the Pacific and whatnot. That's what happened. It was wrong, but I would not be surprised to see it happen again—in time of war. It's no justification, but it is the reality.[26]

Today, a grimmer reality Justice Scalia did not foresee has taken hold in America. War is no longer a necessary pretext for detaining people and violating their basic human rights. Fear and racism are sufficient, and neither public outrage, common sense, nor legal pronouncements appear to be able to stop the actions of a president with imperial aspirations.

Take, for example, President Trump's zero-tolerance policy on America's southern border. Beginning around July 2017, the policy separated parents from children and threw both into cages. It was called "government-sanctioned child abuse" by the president of the American Association of Pediatrics and condemned by the United Nations High Commissioner for Human Rights.[27]

66% of Americans oppose the U.S. policy of separating children and parents when families illegally cross the border into America, but 27% of Americans support it.[28]

Seeming to bow to public outrage, in June 2018 Trump issued an executive order to end such family separations. But according to the American Civil Liberties Union, the U.S. government has quietly continued the separation regime out of the public eye, separating more than 1,100 children from their families between June 2018 and December 2019.[29]

LESSON 11

FEAR BREEDS REPRESSION; REPRESSION BREEDS HATE; HATE MENACES STABLE GOVERNMENT

SENATOR JOE'S ENEMIES FROM WITHIN

Trumpism is not an anomaly in American politics. While it is a more virulent strain of paranoid-style politics, Trump's smear and fear tactics, bullying, lying, and withering attacks on the press, the establishment, Never-Trump Republicans, liberals, and Democrats, as well as his ominous warnings about deep-state conspiracies, are direct descendants of Senator Joseph McCarthy's scorched-earth politics of the 1950s.

Trumpism is McCarthyism on presidential steroids. And it is the great power of the presidency that makes Donald Trump an even more dangerous and existential threat to democracy than McCarthy was seventy years ago.

* * *

Joe McCarthy was not the first political opportunist to use fear and smear tactics for electoral gain. Nor was he the first candidate or elected official to weaponize Red-baiting—accusing someone, typically without evidence, of being sympathetic to communism, affiliating with communists, or being a member of the Communist Party. But McCarthy was the first politician to combine smear campaigning with a complete disdain for institutional norms, civility, and decency. He was a transactional politician, a serial liar who sought political power at any cost.

McCarthy was also a wannabe demagogue whom biographer David M. Oshinsky described as "a soldier of fortune, not an ideologue. Voting conservative, voting liberal—it hardly mattered to him."[1] In his prime, he did the dirty work of the Republican establishment. At first the Republican grandees of the Senate looked the other way, hoping to reap the political benefits of McCarthyism without recognizing its potential costs. But in the end, as McCarthy built a public following that made him impervious to establishment sanctions and virtually uncontrollable, the Senate, America's institutions, and the nation all paid a high price for his demagoguery.

In 1947, 37% of Americans approved of the House Un-American Activities Committee's hearing into "communist infiltration and subversion" in Hollywood. (Asked of the 80% of Americans who said they knew about the hearings.)[2]

McCarthy's transformation from back-bench senator to commie-hunting crusader began in earnest in early 1950. It was driven by political necessity. Young and abrasive, McCarthy had alienated senators on both sides of the aisle when he was first elected to Congress. His punishment, meted out by the power brokers in his own party, was an assignment to serve on the District of Columbia Committee—the political equivalent of a graveyard. McCarthy's falling political status in Washington did not go unnoticed at home. Wisconsin newspapers began openly questioning McCarthy's effectiveness and criticizing his ethics. And rumors of primary opposition to his reelection began to circulate among Republican insiders.

Something dramatic was needed to resuscitate McCarthy's flagging political fortunes. But what would do the trick? There was a tempting road map. In 1947, Republicans had doubled down on their Red-baiting campaign rhetoric by convening hearings of the House Un-American Committee (HUAC) into the infiltration of Hollywood by communists. The hearings, chaired by Republican J. Parnell Thomas of New Jersey and featuring freshmen Republican congressmen like Richard Nixon, were a national sensation and, in conservative circles, a political capital builder.

During the presidential election year of 1948, HUAC moved on to another conservative political pleaser: a witch hunt for Reds in Washington. During its hearings, Republican committee members accused Alger Hiss, a State Department official, of being a communist mole.[3] During hearings and two subsequent trials, Republicans turned Hiss into a symbol of communist treachery and elite New Dealer disdain for America. New Dealers, including Secretary of State Dean Acheson, stood up and defended Hiss from Republican attacks. Hiss maintained his innocence, but when he was convicted of one count of perjury after a second trial in January 1950, the State Department became a ripe target for political attacks. With the communist takeover of China and the Soviet Union's detonation of an atomic bomb in 1949, public fear of communism was rising. The political opportunity presented by commie-hunting—especially for a senator with few scruples and significant political problems—was a no-brainer, and McCarthy seized it like a junkyard dog.

At an event in Wheeling, West Virginia, on February 9, 1950, to celebrate the 141st birthday of Abraham Lincoln, McCarthy began the hunt by warning that "when a great democracy is destroyed, it will not be from enemies from without, but rather because of enemies from within."[4] McCarthy attributed the "enemies from within" language to Lincoln, but as with so much of his rhetoric, the attribution was a fabrication. Though Lincoln's address at the Springfield Young Men's Lyceum in January 1838 conveyed similar sentiments, Lincoln never uttered the words McCarthy ascribed to him.

In the rest of the Wheeling speech, McCarthy argued that America faced an apocalypse—a coming carnage of unprecedented magnitude. America was in a hot war against communism, and it was losing the battle quickly. Using statistics fabricated out of whole cloth, McCarthy warned that in "less than six years" the odds of America defeating the Red threat "have changed from 9 to 1 in our favor to 8 to 5 against us." America was losing the war on communism so swiftly, according to McCarthy, "not because our only powerful potential enemy has sent men to invade our shore . . . but rather because of the traitorous actions of those who have been treated so well by the Nation."[5]

McCarthy alleged that America's enemies were within the American government: They were not real Americans. They were traitors "born with silver spoons in their mouths." In today's parlance, they were the elites of the deep state.

With the enemy within defined as traitorous, deep-state elites, McCarthy then launched his witch hunt. He claimed, "I have here in my hand a list of 57" enemies—"a list of names that were known to the Secretary of State as being members of the Communist Party and who nevertheless are still working and shaping policy in the State Department." It was time to out these traitors and drain the Washington swamp.[6]

To this day, it is unclear how many people were actually on the list in McCarthy's hand, or even the number of Reds McCarthy claimed to identify that day. A printed copy of the speech, handed out to the press before McCarthy spoke, cited 205 communists in the State Department. The next day in Denver, on his way to another speech in Salt Lake City, McCarthy told the press that his list included 207 known commies. (The *Denver Post* ran with McCarthy's claim even though the senator was unable to produce the list for the paper's reporter because, he said, it was locked up in his suitcase on the plane.) In his speech delivered in Salt Lake City, McCarthy claimed that fifty-seven card-carrying communists were working at the State Department.

By the time McCarthy arrived in Reno a day later, the press was waiting for him. McCarthy's charges were gaining traction, and he did not disappoint the assembled reporters, telling them he had sent a telegram to President Truman demanding that the State Department's files be opened for a full inspection by the Senate. Then he went on to deliver another enemies-from-within speech to the Republican faithful waiting for him.

The transcript of the Wheeling speech printed in the *Congressional Record* repeated McCarthy's allegation of fifty-seven communists at the State Department. But on February 20, 1950, in an eight-hour pitched battle on the Senate floor that capped his nation-crossing tour to expose the "enemies within," McCarthy raised the ante to eighty-one communists in the State Department while changing his description of them from card-carrying Reds to loyalty risks.

The number of names on McCarthy's list is immaterial. Facts were not important to McCarthy; he was, in large part, making up his figures on the fly. Capturing headlines, stoking public fear, and building a national political profile and power were McCarthy's goals. Publicizing lists of supposed enemies, smearing people, and seeking a confrontation with President Truman, New Deal Democrats, and anyone else who got in his way were all part of a sensationalist reality show with McCarthy as the star.

By the time McCarthy wrapped up his unhinged presentation on the Senate floor near midnight on February 20 (a performance fellow Republican senator Robert A. Taft described as "perfectly reckless"), McCarthy had taken a significant step toward achieving his goals.[7] He had seized the national spotlight.

Press coverage of McCarthy's accusations forced Senate Democrats to call for additional hearings—the cloud conjured by McCarthy and now hanging over President Truman's State Department had to be dispelled. Full of hubris and misreading the public mood and the media's appetite for McCarthy's red meat, Senate Democrats predicted they would quickly dispense with McCarthy's flimsy accusations.

The additional hearings began on March 8 and dragged on into May. They proved little about the communists' grip on the State Department and disproved even less. But at their conclusion, there was one clear winner: Joe McCarthy. With the public behind him and the political establishment of both parties thoroughly cowed, McCarthy's hunt for commies in Washington had just begun, and a new phrase was coined to describe it: McCarthyism.

In 1950, 46% of Americans familiar with McCarthy's accusation that communists had infiltrated the State Department thought the "charges were doing more good than harm."[8]

With his popularity soaring and the press corps fawning over him, few dared question McCarthy publicly. At a press conference at the end of March, President Truman, answering a reporter's question about the ongoing Senate hearings into traitors in the State Department, stepped into the fray, saying, "I think that the greatest asset the Kremlin has is Senator McCarthy."[9] Realizing his political mistake, Truman quickly reversed course and refused to elaborate further. No one wanted to take on McCarthy.

While others in Washington ducked, one Republican senator, Margaret Chase Smith, was so concerned by McCarthy's demagoguery that she took action. Smith was the only woman in the Senate in 1950. She was also the only senator who had the courage to call out McCarthy on the Senate floor.

A model of civility and bipartisanship, Smith did not name McCarthy directly. That would have been a blatant violation of Senate Rule 19, which prohibits senators from directly or indirectly imputing the conduct or motive of another senator. She did make it abundantly clear, however, whom she was talking about.

Smith began her "Declaration of Conscience" speech on the Senate floor ominously:

I would like to speak briefly and simply about a serious national condition. It is a national feeling of fear and frustration that could result in national suicide and the end of everything that we Americans hold dear. It is a condition that comes from the lack of effective leadership in either the Legislative Branch or the Executive Branch of our Government.

Saying, "I speak as a Republican, I speak as a woman, I speak as a United States Senator. I speak as an American," Smith stripped McCarthyism down to its fundamentals, demonstrating that McCarthy's principles were inimical to Americanism:

Those of us who shout the loudest about Americanism in making character assassinations are all too frequently those who, by our own words and acts, ignore some of the basic principles of Americanism; the right to criticize; the right to hold unpopular beliefs; the right to protest; the right of independent thought.

She concluded with a fusillade directed at both parties:

As an American, I am shocked at the way Republicans and Democrats alike are playing directly into the Communist design of "confuse, divide, and conquer." As an American, I don't want a Democratic Administration "whitewash" or "cover-up" any more than I want a Republican smear or witch hunt. As an American, I condemn a Republican "Fascist" just as much as I condemn a Democratic "Communist." I condemn a Democratic "Fascist" just as much as I condemn a Republican "Communist." They are equally dangerous to you and me and to our country. As an American, I want to see our Nation recapture the strength and unity it once had when we fought the enemy instead of ourselves.[10]

Six senators signed on to Smith's "Declaration of Conscience." But support for her clarion call to purpose and principle ended there. Smith's speech landed with a thud and soon was buried as the war on the Korean peninsula began to take center stage.

With few people in the press, parties, and politics willing to oppose him, McCarthy seared American politics and society for three more years, trampling the Constitution and ruining reputations and lives while feeding public paranoia. The commie fever finally broke in 1954 when McCarthy took on the U.S. Army and President Eisenhower in televised hearings. Without the filter of a fawning press corps, the truth about McCarthy and McCarthyism, of which Senator Smith had warned, was finally on full display for the nation to see. It was captured in one unforgettable televised exchange. With McCarthy on the attack, Attorney Joseph Welch asked: "Have you no sense of decency, sir, at long last? Have you left no sense of decency?"[11] The answer, to anyone watching (and millions of Americans watched the hearings live or in the news roundups broadcast at the end of each day), was obviously no.

According to a Gallup poll, 50 percent of Americans held favorable views of Senator Joe McCarthy in January 1954, with only 29 percent having an unfavorable opinion. By June of 1954, at the conclusion of the Army-McCarthy hearings, McCarthy's favorable rating had fallen to 34 percent and his unfavorable rating stood at 45 percent.

Four years after McCarthy began his Red-baiting campaign and McCarthyism became a household word, senators found the courage and values they had misplaced. On December 2, 1954, with Margaret Chase Smith in the lead, the Senate voted 65 to 22 to censure Joe McCarthy.

CODA

McCarthyism is back. It's now called Trumpism. It pits American against American, erodes the rule of law, and corrodes our values.

Trumpism is flourishing in a media landscape unfiltered by gatekeepers and turned into an echo chamber by bots, social networks, and purveyors of "alternative facts." If it is not challenged and repulsed, it will inexorably destroy our Constitution and American democracy.

Senator Margaret Chase Smith's words in her

"Declaration of Conscience" are a clarion call to us all today:

> I think that it is high time for the United States Senate and its members to do some soul-searching—for us to weigh our consciences—on the manner in which we are performing our duty to the people of America—on the manner in which we are using or abusing our individual powers and privileges. I think that it is high time that we remembered that we have sworn to uphold and defend the Constitution.

LESSON 12

THE SURVEILLANCE SOCIETY AND THE BIG LIE
TOTAL INFORMATION AWARENESS

America's twenty-first-century Pearl Harbor—the attacks on 9/11—was a cathartic public event with political and constitutional ramifications we are still sorting out today.

In the aftermath of the tragedy, the Fourth Amendment's protections against unreasonable searches and seizures and the Fifth and Fourteenth Amendments' due process provisions were sacrificed for security. Ostensibly, these constitutionally guaranteed rights were abridged to protect America from future attacks. But they were junked wholesale without the full knowledge or consent of Americans. As we know all too well, in war the law is silent: constitutional protections are abrogated during wartime, and reestablished when the war ends. That has been our history. But the war that began on 9/11 is different. It is endless. And the constitutional infringements allowed in its aftermath continue today unabated and largely undebated.

In 2014, 22% of Americans said they would sacrifice
civil liberties to be safe from terrorism.

42% of Americans also approved of the government's collection of Americans' phone and internet
data.[1]

The wholesale monitoring of Americans has become a new normal, replacing the pre-9/11 constitutional regime with a surveillance society in which
every American is a suspect and almost everything we
do is monitored, cached, and inspected by a state security apparatus. The result is a United States that has
become a house divided against itself—a constitutional republic choked by a surveillance state rivaling
the most intrusive authoritarian regime. How America became a constitutional republic wrapped in a security state is the story of a secret presidential order,
a program called Total Information Awareness, and a
bait-and-switch sold to Americans by some members
of Congress and a gullible media.

* * *

In the days immediately following 9/11, President
George W. Bush issued a flurry of public proclamations and executive orders. With the stroke of a pen,
Bush declared a national emergency, ordered the
ready reserves of the armed forces to active duty, and
established the Office of Homeland Security. These
public pronouncements were accompanied by secret

presidential orders that still remain under wraps today. One of these orders, uncovered by the *New York Times* four years later, authorized the National Security Agency (NSA) to warrantlessly intercept telephone calls and emails made within the United States—a direct violation of both the Fourth Amendment and the Foreign Intelligence Surveillance Act of 1978. With a green light from the president to ignore Fourth Amendment protections against warrantless search and seizure, the NSA began a program of surreptitious snooping into the private conversations and communications of Americans far and wide.[2]

NSA was not the only government agency working to increase the intelligence-gathering capabilities of the U.S. government on American soil. Just four months after 9/11, the Department of Defense established the Information Awareness Office (IAO) in the Defense Advanced Research Projects Agency to "create the tools that would permit analysts to data-mine an indefinitely expandable universe of databases."[3]

The official seal of the IAO is a conspiracy theorist's dream—an all-seeing eye on the apex of a pyramid scanning what appears to be a globe (take a look at the back of the dollar bill in your pocket for the logo's doppelganger). The resemblance to symbols associated with the Illuminati is hard to miss and makes any sane person wonder: Who comes up with this stuff, anyway?

Retired admiral John Poindexter was tapped to run the IAO. Poindexter left the navy after he was indicted, along with Lieutenant Colonel Oliver North, for his role in the Iran-Contra affair. Poindexter was convicted on five counts of lying to Congress about the illicit arms sales to Iran that generated dirty dollars to fund the Contras fighting Marxists in Nicaragua—an illegal circumvention of Congress and U.S. foreign policy. On appeal, Poindexter's conviction was overturned. He avoided jail and exchanged government service for government contracting, landing at BMT Syntek Technologies, a defense contractor in DARPA's employ that was developing a data-mining system called Project Genoa.

IAO's mission was to "develop new tools to detect, anticipate, train for, and provide warnings about potential terrorist attacks"—certainly a worthy goal.[4] As part of its mission, IAO begat the Total Information Awareness (TIA) program. And under Poindexter's lead, TIA set about integrating Project Genoa with a host of ongoing programs with creepy names like Genisys, Bio-Surveillance, Evidence Extraction and Link Discovery, Communicator, and Babylon, with the aim of developing a cohesive intelligence-gathering and -sifting operation.

Poindexter's goal for TIA was ambitious: to "help analysts search randomly for indications of travel to risky areas, suspicious emails, odd fund transfers, and improbable medical activity."[5] To facilitate the back-up-the-dump-truck approach of this random search, "a database 'of an unprecedented scale,'" including information from public and private data holdings, would be developed "to obtain transactional and biometric data" on all Americans.[6] In short, Poindex-ter's TIA was gearing up to gather, warehouse, and sift through public and private information on every American without probable cause or warrants. In essence, TIA would ransack and inspect Americans' laundry and underwear drawer continuously, indis-criminately, and forever in search of suspicious activity.

It is hard to imagine a more intrusive, authoritar-ian governmental program. Under TIA, all Americans were suspect and watched by an all-seeing, all-knowing eye, much like in the IAO logo. TIA was Orwell's Big Brother on digital steroids.

On November 9, 2002, the *New York Times* gave Americans a glimpse of the DOD's plans for TIA. The overview was alarming:

> The Pentagon is constructing a computer system that could create a vast electronic dragnet, search-ing for personal information as part of the hunt for terrorists around the globe—including the United States. . . . Historically, military and intelligence agencies have not been permitted to spy on Ameri-cans without extraordinary legal authorization. But Admiral Poindexter, the former national security adviser in the Reagan administration, has argued that the government needs broad new powers to process, store, and mine billions of minute details of electronic life in the United States.[7]

Once TIA's goals became public, the reaction against it was swift. Protecting America by continually collecting and analyzing the private information of every American was reviled as an unconstitutional invasion antithetical to liberty and freedom. The price for the absolute security promised by TIA was simply too high. The public and the media objected to TIA as "a massive and unjustified governmental intrusion into the personal lives of Americans."[8]

A year after TIA was established within the Defense Department, Congress began oversight hearings. By September 2003, with great fanfare, Congress terminated the TIA's funding in the fiscal year 2004 Department of Defense appropriations act and dismantled the IAO.

Defenders of the Constitution in Congress and the public celebrated. They shouldn't have. The story that Congress slew the surveillance society dragon was a big lie—a lie that is still at work today.

TIA was not killed by Congress. Through legislative legerdemain, it was secretly moved from the public budget of the United States to the "black budget," through which the clandestine programs of the national security state are funded.

To the public and the press, TIA was terminated. To the security state, "funding for TIA's component technologies" was preserved and "transferred to other government agencies" with only one legislative proviso as a fig leaf: it could not be used for spying on American citizens.[9]

The secret order issued by President Bush immediately after 9/11 made that sole legislative restriction on TIA technology toothless. That order was issued pursuant to the Authorization to Use Military Force (AUMF) passed by Congress on September 14, 2001. (The AUMF is still in force today—a legacy of America's endless war.) It authorizes the "use [of] all necessary and appropriate force" to prevent terrorist attacks on the United States. The data-mining and other TIA capabilities acquired by the NSA allow it to indiscriminately sweep up information on Americans, enable facial recognition, track biometrics, and eavesdrop on your phone calls and emails—and the NSA is excused from following the probable-cause protections of the Fourth Amendment because the information gathered is used to identify possible terrorists. President Bush's order empowers the security state to ignore the Constitution in order to find the few terrorist needles lurking in the large haystack that is the American public.

With the AUMF, Bush's secret order, and a compliant Department of Justice, the NSA had the authority, additional technology, and budget to build and operate a mass surveillance system on Americans, even though most Americans opposed it.

The NSA mass surveillance system, at least what we know of it, is called PRISM. Edward Snowden spilled the beans on it and is still paying the price for what some call treason and others say is patriotism. While Congress ostensibly pulled the plug on the NSA's archiving of Americans' phone calls in 2015, other PRISM and PRISM-like surveillance programs continue unabated. And in August 2019, President Trump and his administration, claiming that the present surveillance capacities of the security state were inadequate, asked Congress to approve a new, reconfigured spying program.

CODA

The NSA and other intelligence agencies' wholesale snooping on Americans is another example of "destroying the village in order to save it." Unlike the Vietnam War, during which this phrase was first coined to describe the devastation of Ben Tre by the U.S. military, this time the village is our country, and what we are destroying, or at least abridging, are some of the fundamental constitutional protections on which America was founded.

Congress and America's security state played ordinary Americans. The programs defunded by Congress in the public budget were quietly moved to the black budget, and they remain there today, legacies of the 9/11 attacks. Almost two decades later, they operate in the shadows, unchecked except in classified briefings by oversight committees. Today, Americans have no right to know how, when, where, and how regularly our government rifles through our "persons, houses, papers, and effects."[10]

Secret orders, secret transfers of power, and unabashed lying to the American people are examples of a government and system that do not respect the Constitution and our rights as citizens. Madison, Hamilton, Franklin, Washington, and the other founders of

America would be appalled at the surveillance society that has metastasized across America since 9/11.

Americans cannot hold our government accountable if we do not know what our government is doing. In a democracy, the government acts with the consent of the people. In an authoritarian state, or one on its way to authoritarianism, the government acts without the knowledge or consent of the people and legitimizes its action by contending, *We know better.*

A government of, by, and for the people cannot exist when the people are kept in the dark. The *Washington Post*'s official slogan is spot-on: "Democracy dies in darkness."

Fear of serious injury cannot alone justify suppression of free speech and assembly. Men feared witches and burnt women. It is the function of speech to free men from the bondage of irrational fears.

—Justice Louis Brandeis, *Whitney v. California* (1927)

CONCLUSION

POGO WAS WRONG!

FEAR, POLARIZATION, THE 1619 PROJECT, AND TEN STEPS TO STRENGTHEN AMERICA

> We have met the enemy, and he is us.
> —Pogo

We are not the enemy. Fear is the enemy—whether it's fear of liberals, conservatives, gays, straights, transgender individuals, feminists, blacks, Muslims, whites, Native Americans, Latinos, immigrants, *Mayflower* descendants, Dreamers, Daughters of the American Revolution, card-carrying members of the ACLU, card-carrying NRA members, Fox News aficionados, or anyone who is an American citizen or shares America's values. Fear dupes some of us into demanding uniformity over diversity and permits too many of us to turn our backs on the motto inscribed on the Great Seal of our Republic in 1782: *e pluribus unum*.

Fear activates the reservoir of intolerance that resides dormant within many Americans on the right, on the left, and in the center. (The reserve of bigotry and narrow-mindedness is documented at the beginning of this book by the Index of American Authoritarian Attitudes.)

It is also the wellspring of what historian Rogers Smith calls America's ascriptive tradition. The ascriptive tradition is an anathema to America's founding precepts. It contends "that the nation's political and economic structures should formally reflect natural and cultural inequalities, even at the cost of violating doctrines of universal rights."[1] It serves as a secret escape clause from the aspiration that all people are created equal and should be treated as such.

As Madison warned us in Federalist 63, self-interested people have used fear to enflame our violent passions and shape American history to their will. They did so in the late eighteenth century, and they are doing so again today. Their successes, and our failures to live up to the promise of America, have occasioned some of the darkest moments of our past and present.

We need only to remember our history, or read one of the most significant Supreme Court dissents ever written, to know where fear can lead: "Fear breeds repression, repression breeds hate, hate menaces stable government." Never forget: "Men feared witches and burnt women."[2]

Fear is a fearsome enemy of democracy and American exceptionalism. It is behind the stark polarization that divides America today, both politically and socially. Wielded by self-interested political and media elites, it makes discussion, debate, and compromise about public issues virtually impossible and transforms citizens with whom we disagree into enemies. Polarization is so deep in America today we can't even have a constructive public dialogue about slavery without shouting smears and retreating into predictable and deeply defended corners.

When in 2019 the *New York Times* launched its 1619 Project to explore the long shadow slavery cast on American history and the role black Americans have played in building the country and perfecting the Constitution, the response from the intolerant right was rage. Pundits smeared the project and stoked fears about its real purpose. They warned that the 1619 Project was propaganda, an attempt to brainwash Americans and rewrite American history.

Our history, they argued, can only be understood from one perspective, "our perspective"—which in this case is the lens of the ascriptive tradition and the hegemony of white America. Under that lens, the experience of blacks in America and their contributions to the country are irrelevant, immaterial, and unimportant to understanding American history.

The enraged response to the 1619 Project is symptomatic of the political polarization that is tearing America apart today piece by piece—a polarization that has moved beyond the political sphere to infect society and is now corrupting even basic understandings of the rules governing our polity, and what is and is not a fact.

America's democracy is not likely to survive extreme political and social polarization exacerbated by disagreements over fundamental rules and facts.

When the loyal opposition becomes a political and social enemy, a foe who no longer shares "our values" or "our understanding of reality," opponents become the other—outsiders with no standing in society who no longer deserve protection under the law. They are the enemy within; their otherness justifies cutting constitutional corners and restricting civil liberties to protect us from them.

The path we are on right now in America leads to a hollowing out of our Republic. It will result in the rise of a democracy in name only, where elections do not have consequences and the rule of law is replaced by the law of the powerful. It is a sad and unworthy answer to Benjamin Franklin's prescient challenge issued at the end of the Constitutional Convention in 1787. Instead of keeping the Republic, we will have lost it.

The job of each one of us—regardless of our ideology and party—is to take personal responsibility for the health and strength of our democracy, our aspirational values, and our system of government. We can no longer rely on elites, institutions, and unelected gatekeepers to do the job for us, because they aren't. We can't expect other citizens to do the work either. It will take most of us, united and working together, to get our country back on the right path. And we can't count on simple solutions or slogans to magically do the job. Calling for or supporting some vaguely defined "revolution" is an irresponsible and reckless response—a knee-jerk, facile answer whose more likely outcome is authoritarianism, not renewed democracy, equality, and civil society.

To strengthen our Republic, we must reject the traps of fear, polarization, and hate set time and again by the self-serving fearmongering of self-interested people, because that leads to repression and fascism. Instead, we must recommit to advancing the fundamental principles on which America was founded. It is through our work that these principles can be perfected. That is our inheritance as Americans. Will we squander it or strengthen it?

TEN STEPS TO STRENGTHEN AMERICA

There are ten steps each one of us can take starting today to strengthen America. These steps aren't easy, and they are certainly not all we need to do. But they are a way forward that each one of us can commit to doing.

The first five steps come from James Madison's writing and are what he saw as the five necessary and sufficient conditions for maintaining a strong Republic, published five years after the Constitutional Convention and written with the acknowledgment "that in 'every political society, parties are unavoidable.'"[3]

Madison's first necessary condition is to "establish political equality among all." Even though Madison's definition of "all" was most likely limited to white males, the notion of political equality was a radical idea in 1792. (Given the state of contemporary politics in America, it appears to be just as subversive a concept today.) For democracy to flourish, establishing and maintaining equality for all is a condition that must be met without qualification. We cannot attain it by supporting equality only for those who look and think like us, offering everyone else something much less. Political equality for all means that every citizen has an equal voice and stake in America because each one of us is the equal of the others. We don't play games with some people's right to vote, with the enforcement of laws, with facts, or with the rights to speech, assembly, religion, and privacy. The Constitution, with its Bill of Rights and due process and equal protection clauses, applies to everyone equally, and with those equal rights comes an individual responsibility to fellow citizens, our community, and our country.

Madison's second through fourth necessary conditions for maintaining a healthy Republic are equality of opportunity, economic equality, and the prohibition of special deals for powerful special interests. Madison calls for "withholding unnecessary opportunities for a few," which "increase the inequality of property, by an immoderate, and especially unmerited, accumulation of riches [second condition]." He argues for "the silent operation of laws, which, without violating the rights of property, reduce extreme wealth towards a state of mediocrity, and raise extreme indigence towards a state of comfort [third condition]." And he advocates for a ban on "measures which operate differently on different interests, and particularly such as favor one interest, at the expense of another [fourth condition]."

If Madison were alive today and articulated these principles, it is more than likely that some would smear him as a socialist. That is how far debate in

America has strayed from our founding principles. Undoubtedly, Madison would see America's increasing economic inequality and our government's many giveaways to special-interest elites and wannabe oligarchs as violations of all three of these conditions. What would Madison do about this? He'd take to the streets and use the ballot box to change our government and make it do the business of the people.

The fifth and final condition Madison cites as necessary for democracy is "making one party a check on the other, so far as the existence of parties cannot be prevented." Party competition regulated by constitutional checks and balances is central to the maintenance of democracy. Implicit in this condition is the need for compromise within an established set of rules and an agreed-upon set of norms. When elected officials and others willfully violate or ignore these norms, disregard their responsibilities, break constitutional oaths, and pursue winner-take-all political outcomes at any cost, democracy is imperiled.

The next five steps we can each take are the lessons that flow from the American history examined in these pages and the history we are all living through each day.

Sixth: For America to be strong and become exceptional, Americans must stop othering each other. We need to stop the fearmongering and name-calling. No more labeling one another as a "libtard," "snowflake," or "deplorable." No more reveling in the drawing of differences between us and them, or the superiority of our group or opinion over another.

If we pledge ourselves to the equality that Madison claims is a necessary condition for democracy to exist, then each one of our fellow countrymen and -women deserves respect and the right to be heard. Fearmongers thrive by fomenting disunity. When we mimic them, we are tearing down America, not building it up. We need to get out of our bubbles and our highly defended corners and start listening to the people with whom we disagree. America's real enemy is not the American we disagree with. There is no "enemy within"—except the self-interested misleaders who exacerbate our problems. Our real enemy is ignorance and the lure of simple authoritarian answers to complex problems.

Seventh: Americans need to confront and make peace with our history. We have much to be proud of as Americans, but we also have a history that needs to be confronted, understood, and exorcised. Denial of our mistakes compounds them. Reconciliation of our past transgressions strengthens us as a people. Reconciling our past begins by acknowledging the people who have lacked power in America and listening intently to their voices.

Eighth: As we make peace with our past, we also need to confront and understand the challenges our fellow citizens face. Fear is a growing factor in American politics today because many people are afraid of what the next day will bring. Will they be able to pay their bills? Will they lose their job? Will their children have the opportunity to succeed in the world? Are they safe when they walk down the street? Will they be listened to? Does their country care about them? Why are they being left behind? The hurt in America today is as great as the hurt in America's past that needs to be reconciled. We will not move ahead as a nation unless we listen and work to resolve both.

Ninth: We need to recommit ourselves to the proposition that there are objective facts and that these facts must shape how our country makes decisions. The snake-oil sellers pushing alternative facts, conspiracy theories, and ersatz science do not care about making America stronger; they care about making themselves wealthier and more powerful. Their lies are geared to manipulate, stoke fear, and shape a gullible public to their liking. Our job as citizens in a democracy—and our responsibility—is to sort out the fabrications and identify the facts. If you want to live in a democracy, you simply have to take the time to do this.

Tenth and finally: We need to remember something that has been forgotten by too many, which is that we are all in this together. Service to each other and our country must become a requirement of citizenship. Military service, community service, service to others—everyone must give back to our nation in one way or another for a year or more. There can be no exceptions, no deferments, no special deals, no bone spurious excuses. All in. All together. All Americans working for their country.

Each of us taking ten steps to strengthen America may seem like a bridge too far—a Pollyannaish prescription for a Mad Max world. It is not. It is what is necessary to protect and defend our birthright as Americans. I think it is worth protecting and perfecting. And I find myself in good company.

Senator Margaret Chase Smith knew how important it was to protect our birthright. In 1950 she took a stand to do so. Even though her Senate colleagues ignored her "Declaration of Conscience" at first, history revealed that her words were prescient. Here is how she concluded that declaration:

> It is high time that we stopped thinking politically as Republicans and Democrats about elections and started thinking patriotically as Americans about national security based on individual freedom. It is high time that we all stopped being tools and victims of totalitarian techniques—techniques that, if continued here unchecked, will surely end what we have come to cherish as the American way of life.[4]

MEASURING COMMITMENT
TO DEMOCRACY

I spend a lot of my waking hours deep in data, testing hypotheses and trying to understand people's answers to survey questions. One set of five questions that I find particularly revealing asks people the following about preferences for different types of political systems.

Here are the questions. (Add up your score as you go along!)

First, do you think army rule is a very good, somewhat good, somewhat bad, or very bad way to govern the United States?

If you answered "somewhat bad" or "very bad," you earn one point.

Second, would you say a democratic political system is a very good, somewhat good, somewhat bad, or very bad way to govern the United States?

This time, if you answered "very good" or "somewhat good," give yourself another point.

Next, is having a strong leader who does not have to bother with Congress and elections a very good, somewhat good, somewhat bad, or very bad way to govern the United States?

If you answered "somewhat bad" or "very bad," add another point to your total.

Changing question formats now, which of these statements is closest to your view? **A.** Democracy is preferable to any other kind of government. **B.** In some circumstances, a nondemocratic government can be preferable. **C.** For someone like me, it doesn't matter what kind of government we have.

If you chose statements A or C, you earned another point.

Finally, on a 1-to-10 scale—where 1 represents "not at all important" and 10 is "very important"—how important is it for you to live in a country that is governed democratically?

If you answered 8 or above, you get one last point to add to your total score.

Your score should range between 0 and 5.
What does your score mean?
These five questions have been asked for years in different combinations in surveys taken in the United

States and around the world to gauge public support for democracy and democratic institutions. In 2018, a group of researchers from the Democracy Fund Voter Study Group aggregated them into what they argue is a measure of support for democratic government. In their methodology, a score of 5 indicates consistent support for democracy, while a score below 5 indicates an openness "to illiberal appeals when foreign and domestic actors are actively seeking to subvert our democratic institutions."

Another way to think about these questions is as a measurement of potential—the potential for undemocratic forms of government to grow and take hold in a country. Anyone scoring below 5 is more likely to support cutting democratic corners when they are told, or are scared enough to believe, it is necessary.

What is this potential in the United States? When I ask this question in my travels around America, most people guess that somewhere between 66 and 90 percent of Americans are consistent supporters of democracy—a 5 on the scale. That hopeful guess is woefully mistaken. Only 54 percent of Americans score a perfect 5 on the democracy quiz. Forty-six percent of our fellow countrywomen and -men are not strong, patriotic supporters of democracy, and almost a third (31 percent) would not mind in the least having our government run by a strong leader who doesn't have to pay attention to Congress and elections.

Consistent support for democracy is the first item

on the Index of American Authoritarian Attitudes. Its estimate of Americans' lack of support for the very form of government we extol and hold out as the proof of our exceptionalism is as eye-opening as the thirteen other items that round out the index and form the starting point for *On Fascism*.

CAUSALITY AND
AUTHORITARIANISM

Causality is another concept that is vitally important to understanding the centrality of activated authoritarianism in America today.

Like many others, I contend that authoritarianism sits at the beginning of a causal chain from which other behaviors can develop. As such, an inclination to authoritarianism can then influence the development of racism, sexism, nativism, nationalism, and all the other isms that have been blamed for the recent rise of illiberal politics on both sides of the Atlantic.

In this accounting, the question of which came first, the chicken or the egg, is settled. Authoritarianism came first. It is the taproot of intolerance—an instinctive yearning for uniformity that predisposes people to bigoted behaviors that are socially and culturally constructed. It is not only correlated with attitudes like sexism and racism but occurs before them and affects their development.

That is the theory. Authoritarian scholars defend

it tooth and nail. But do the questions regarding child-rearing that I use to estimate a person's disposition toward authoritarianism accurately capture this critical temporal distinction between authoritarianism and all the other isms on which the theory rests?

To help answer this, consider a question: Growing up, which of the following did you form an opinion about first? Did you form an opinion about *respecting your parents and grandparents*, or did you develop an attitude about *illegal immigrants posing a threat to public safety*?

I suspect most of you chose respecting your parents. In other words, you learned about respecting elders well before you developed any opinions about illegal immigrants and safety.

Now, how about this question: Did you form an attitude about *obedience to authority* first, or an opinion about *whether women seek to gain power by getting control over men*? Again, I bet you learned to follow your parents' orders (or at least to pretend to follow them) well before you had any view about women trying to control men.

Next, did you learn about *good manners* before you formed an opinion about *racist stereotypes like the inherent laziness of black Americans*? How about when you formed an opinion one way or the other about *an inborn penchant for violence among Muslims*?

Last, how about being well behaved as a child? Did you have an inkling about what it meant to be *well behaved* before you formed an opinion about *whether the system was stacked against people like you?*

On each of these questions, most people form an opinion about the child-rearing value well before the other attitudes in question.

Now, I didn't pick these other attitudinal questions out of the ether. Each one of them comes from polling batteries used to measure enmity toward illegal immigrants, hostile sexism, racial resentment, and populism.

For instance, when a social scientist claims someone is a populist, she is basing that assessment on answers to a battery of questions, and quite likely one of the items asked about is whether the person thinks the system is stacked against them. Like the child-rearing value questions developed to estimate authoritarianism, these are standard questions used to approximate different behaviors. Unlike the disposition approximated by the child-rearing questions, the attitudes estimated by the nativism, sexism, racism, and populism items are formed later in life.

Theoretically, authoritarianism is extant before these other attitudes. Empirically, our authoritarian estimation device—the child-rearing questions—meets this theoretical requirement, measuring opinions that form before other bigoted and intolerant attitudes.

Certainly, the child-rearing questions are not perfect estimators of authoritarianism. Social science is a messy pursuit. But the scale generated from the questions is predictive of a wide range of behaviors associated with authoritarianism, and the questions themselves conform to the temporal demands of authoritarian theory. As measured empirically by the child-rearing battery of questions and stipulated by theory, authoritarianism does develop before the other isms driving politics today, including partisanship and ideology.

The theoretical claim that authoritarianism exists "causally prior to the variables it affects" may not seem important, but it is a very big deal.[1] It implies that authoritarianism has both direct and indirect effects on behaviors like voting for Donald Trump in the United States or Marine Le Pen in France or Matteo Salvini in Italy. Statistical models that fail to take both of these effects into account underestimate the importance of authoritarianism to the outcome.

APPENDIX 3

AUTHORITARIANISM: DEFINITION, STUDY, AND MEASUREMENT

Authoritarianism is a concept with a long and complicated history.

Philosopher and political theorist Isaiah Berlin traced the origins of the modern authoritarian fascism found today in America and elsewhere to the moralist and devout Roman Catholic Joseph de Maistre.[1] After the French Revolution, Maistre became an uncompromising proponent of order, authority, and monarchy. His philosophy is the authoritarian ying to the Enlightenment's yang, "a full-scale attack on reason as preached by the eighteenth century philosophes" that Maistre leveled with the "power and the gusto of the great revolutionaries themselves."[2]

Submission to authority, the maintenance of tradition and order, and aggression toward enemies (others) were the core tenets of Maistre's authoritarian worldview. In this view, obedience to "the terror of authority" is mankind's savior, limiting our freedoms and choices while protecting us from ruinous individualism, intellectualism, and the unceasing assertion of universal rights.[3] "The binding force of custom and tradition" clearly delineates right from wrong, good from evil, and the rules that must be followed to protect order.[4] Transgressors of these rules are a threat—violators of conventions and well-demarcated group boundaries. They are the enemy whose challenge to authority is dangerous and must be confronted and repulsed.

Maistre labeled the enemy of authority and order "la secte," which can be translated as "the faction."[5] This included "the disturbers and subverters . . . all those who throw dust in the eyes of the people or seek to subvert the appointed order."[6] It is almost as if Maistre were writing the script for twenty-first-century autocratic wannabes when he listed the enemies of order: "Jews . . . scientists and democrats . . . liberals . . . idealists, lawyers, journalists, secular reformers, and intellectuals of every breed."[7]

Maistre was indeed "a remarkable, and terrifying, prophet of our day."[8] To Maistre, these enemies of authority must not be tolerated. They "must be rooted out at all costs."[9] How? Aggression is the remedy of choice in Maistre's philosophy, as it is in authoritarian theory.

The study of the behaviors, attitudes, and activation of authoritarian followers by a strongman leader began with the work of the scholars of the Frankfurt Institut fur Sozialforschung (the Institute for Social Research). The Institute, known colloquially as the Frankfurt School, was founded in 1923 and led by

German philosopher and historian Carl Grünberg. A think tank of Jewish, Marxist intellectuals attached to a premier German university was an anathema to the increasingly powerful National Socialists. Within weeks of Hitler taking power, the Nazis seized the institute's library, and its scholars fled to Switzerland, Scandinavia, and eventually the United States. The psychologist Erich Fromm was one of the Frankfurt School's scholars who ended up in America.

In 1941, Fromm published what is recognized as one of the founding works of political psychology and authoritarian studies, *Escape from Freedom*. In this book Fromm advanced a compelling account of why people willingly submit to authoritarian leaders. His explanation was steeped both in the theories of Sigmund Freud and in his first-person observations of the rise of Nazism in Germany.

Fromm's *Escape* is a data-free, historically and theoretically rooted analysis of authoritarianism. It argues that the modern world of the Enlightenment and Industrial Revolution "freed man from traditional authorities" (the authorities Maistre believed were central to humankind's salvation).[10] Modernization led to freedom, but it also led many to feel isolated, insecure, and powerless. Increasing social or economic upheaval and instability fed these fears, transforming freedom into a burden, a risk that became too heavy for some to bear. Some people, especially those inclined to authoritarianism, sought shelter from danger by escaping from freedom. Fear tempted them "to surrender freedom to dictators of all kinds," whose authority promised order and stability in exchange.[11] Submission and obedience to authority provided certainty, security, and shelter from the vagaries of change. It was a trade-off that, Fromm observed, many were all too ready to make.

Fromm considered the flight from freedom to autocratic leadership a systemic threat to democracy.[12] He warned that the forces igniting this fear were not constrained by national borders. People in any modernizing country were exposed to them and could be impelled to escape from freedom.

After Fromm published *Escape from Freedom*, an interdisciplinary team of four social scientists from the Frankfurt School and the University of California at Berkeley was created to examine more thoroughly the psychology of prejudice, intolerance, and anti-Semitism. Like Fromm, the team's research was steeped in theory. Unlike Fromm, the team used data to test their hypotheses. Nine years later, the result was a sprawling, data-packed tour de force called *The Authoritarian Personality: Studies in Prejudice*, which filled the empirical vacuum left by Fromm and "was considered," according to psychologist Franz Samelson, "a milestone in the history of American social psychology."[13]

Fromm's *Escape from Freedom* and *The Authoritarian Personality: Studies in Prejudice* are the theoretical and empirical wells from which the study of authoritarianism sprang. Eighty years after the term "authoritarian character" was first coined, only the Freudian dimensions of authoritarian theory have been completely cast aside. The study of authoritarianism remains interdisciplinary, stretching across sociology, psychology, and political science with new, important avenues of inquiry in epigenetics. Surveys of public opinion are the standard tool for measuring an individual's disposition to authoritarianism and examining the behaviors and attitudes associated with it. Qualitative interviews with authoritarians—individually and in group settings—are used to add important context to the data harvested from surveys. And many researchers today (including me) use a standardized set of four child-rearing questions, which are close descendants of those developed by Frankfurt scholars, to estimate an individual's disposition to authoritarianism.

Typically, these four questions are introduced to survey takers with this short preamble:

Although there are a number of qualities that people believe children should have, every person thinks that some qualities are more important than others. Below are four pairs of desirable qualities.

Then subjects are asked, "Which quality from each pair is more important for a child to have?" The pairs are:

- Respect for elders *or* independence
- Self-reliance *or* obedience
- Good manners *or* curiosity
- Being considerate *or* being well behaved[14]

Respect for elders, obedience, good manners, and being well behaved are the authoritarian answers in each pair. People who select all four of these answers are those who are most likely to be disposed to authoritarianism. On a simple scale built from the answers to these questions, which ranges from 0 (non-authoritarian) to 1 (authoritarian), these people earn a perfect score of 1. Those who select none of the authoritarian answers are placed at the 0 point on the scale. Everyone else fits somewhere in between.

The four questions are simple and parsimonious. They are also a powerful tool for scaling authoritarianism at an individual level. Whether you are American or Dutch, German or French, Italian or Polish, your relative disposition to authoritarianism can be estimated by asking these basic questions about child-rearing.

We know this because the questions are also highly predictive time and again of authoritarian behavior. By "predictive," we mean that the more authoritarian someone is on the scale, the more likely he or she is to behave as theory tells us an authoritarian should behave.

How should authoritarians behave? Theoretically, they should be more likely to dislike certain immigrant groups, favor force over diplomacy, and prefer security over civil rights. They should prefer the edicts of strong leaders over established constitutional protections, choose nationalism over globalism, and be more likely to hold racist, ethnocentric, and sexist views. And, as I have found in America and across Europe, authoritarians are less likely to support democracy.

This is not a definitive list of authoritarian behaviors, but it is a good start. And on survey question after question, these are the exact behaviors authoritarians are more likely to display. Statistically speaking, the more authoritarian people are, according to their answers to the child-rearing questions, the more likely they are to exhibit authoritarian attitudes.

As Mark Hetherington and Jonathan Weiler explain, the child-rearing questions "prompt respondents to choose between a preference for self-directed decision making and [a] strict adherence to the rules."[15] These are choices that theorists from Erich Fromm to cognitive linguist George Lakoff agree are "critical to distinguishing authoritarians from nonauthoritarians."[16]

The questions are also neatly divorced from the behaviors that theory predicts authoritarians should exhibit, enabling researchers, as political scientist Karen Stenner notes, "to distinguish authoritarian predisposition from authoritarian 'products' (attitudes)."[17]

Being predictive, however, is not the same as being deterministic. Not everyone who scores a 1 on the scale behaves like an authoritarian. (By the way, I score a .75.) Conversely, those of you who scored a 0 on the scale should not feel virtuous. Some nonauthoritarians are anything but paragons of enlightened behavior.

The ability of child-rearing value questions to predict seemingly unrelated authoritarian political attitudes and behaviors in the United States and Europe is remarkable, but it is not divination. It is science rooted in theory, quantitative data analysis, and qualitative observations.

Consider for a moment this quote about authority, punishment, respect, and child-rearing that comes from Jack, an American authoritarian I interviewed.[18] In response to a simple question about respecting elders, Jack said:

> I believe respect comes out of a little slap on the ass every once in a while. Excuse my French. If you think about an animal like a dog, if you get a dog as a pup, when you train him—when he does something wrong, he gets punished. When he does something good, you praise him. You talk to him like a human being, not like an animal, and the dog respects you. For the rest of your life the dog will respect you; a child is the same way. I hate to compare a kid with an animal, but it is the same way. When a child does something wrong, they are supposed to be punished for it. You have to stick to the punishment.

Jack's attitude is well formed and articulated. It is also deeply felt. There is little doubt about where Jack sits on the child-rearing continuum between democratic and authoritarian. Jack's comparison of child-rearing to dog training is inarguably a dead giveaway. Just as his earlier answers to the four child-rearing questions I posed before we started talking predicted, Jack is an authoritarian.

While the child-rearing questions are remarkably useful for estimating authoritarianism, they certainly are not perfect. They capture three of the central personality traits of authoritarianism—obedience, conventionalism, and aggression—but one critical dimension remains missing. That missing link is group identification and the feeling of groupness that comes with it.

Enmity toward outgroups—especially threatening outgroups—is an innate human trait. Some researchers think that outgroup threat reinforces in-group identity, exacerbates hostility toward the other, and plays an important causal role in activating authoritarianism.[19] To test this theory, I added questions from what is known as the Social Dominance Orientation battery to estimate individuals' attitudes toward in-group identity and dominance. The questions I included ask whether people agree or disagree on a 7-point scale with two statements:

- Whether some groups deserve to be on top, while other groups deserve to be on the bottom
- If some groups are simply inferior to others

I added the answers to these questions to the child-rearing items to produce a refined measurement of authoritarianism that included group dominance. Then I tested this new tool against the standard authoritarian scale to determine which one was a better predictor of authoritarian behaviors. In all thirteen countries where I tried this experiment so far, the predictability of the child-rearing questions was supersized by the addition of the two group dominance questions.[20]

This new scale, one that includes both child-rearing and group dominance questions, is the measurement I now use to explore the attitudes and voting behaviors of authoritarians in the United States, Europe, and Eurasia.

The scale captures the *Weltanschauung* of the followers of Trumpism and the illiberal elites in Europe mistakenly dubbed "populist." It is what George Lakoff is talking about when he says many of Trump's supporters were simply casting votes "for their worldview."[21] The worldview of authoritarians, activated by the tweets of a self-interested agitator, can lead authoritarians to choose to escape the responsibilities of freedom and follow the leader.

ACKNOWLEDGMENTS

The provenance of a book always appears certain. The reality is: It is not. A long list of people contributed to the ideas in these pages. I thank them all while recognizing a few in particular: Brian Schaffner, Tatishe Nteta, John Brigham, and Sheldon Goldman for their generous mentorship and exceptional scholarship; and Marc Hetherington and Jonathan Weiler for their groundbreaking work on American authoritarianism and boundless collegiality.

This book would have never seen the light of day without the help of Gillian MacKenzie, my exceptional agent, and Pronoy Sarkar, an insightful editor committed to excellence.

The Proteus Fund provided funding for all three American Survey Research Project polls that form the basis of the American Authoritarian Index. Jill Price Marshall, Beery Adams, and George Holt at Proteus added their support and professionalism to the project's vision and management. The University of

Massachusetts Amherst also generously contributed funding for the surveys. And Samantha Luks of You-Gov expertly managed the fielding of the surveys.

Throughout the last several years, Christal More-house has contributed greatly to the study of authoritarianism in the United States and Europe. Her thought partnership and hard work are greatly admired. My long-standing and kindly irascible friend, Don Sanders, helped me maintain perspective and a sense a humor through the early stages of writing this book. Unfortunately, he left this Earth before the manuscript was completed.

Finally, my partner in life, Leah K. Glasheen, provided unflagging support to me during the entire project. This book would not have been started or finished without her. Any mistakes and errors in the book are mine. I apologize to my readers for each and everyone one of them.

NOTES

INTRODUCTION

1. American Survey Research Project, "Three National Panel Surveys."
2. Fromm's classic political psychology text on authoritarianism/fascism is *Escape from Freedom* (New York: Farrar and Rinehart, 1941).
3. Abraham Lincoln, "To Albert G. Hodges," in *The Collected Works of Abraham Lincoln Volume VII*, ed. Roy P. Basler et al. (New Brunswick, NJ: Rutgers University Press, 1953), 281.
4. *Dred Scott v. Sandford*, 60 U.S. (19 How.) 393 (1857), majority opinion by Justice Taney.
5. "Federalist 63, The Senate Continued," The Federalist Papers, Congress.gov Resources, accessed June 12, 2019, https://guides.loc.gov/federalist-papers/text-61-70.
6. See Michelle Alexander, *The New Jim Crow* (New York: New Press, 2010).
7. "Hate Groups Reach Record High," Southern Poverty Law Center, accessed June 15, 2019, https://www.splcenter.org/news/2019/02/19/hate-groups-reach-record-high.
8. Quoted in Daniel Okrent, *The Guarded Gate: Bigotry, Eugenics, and the Law That Kept Two Generations of Jews, Italians, and Other European Immigrants Out of America* (New York: Scribner, 2019), 169. To his credit, in this

speech Smith bravely shredded the hateful notion of scientific racism at the heart of eugenics.

9. Francis Fukuyama, "The End of History?," *National Interest*, no. 16 (Summer 1989): 3–18.

10. "From John Adams to John Taylor, 17 December 1814," *Founders Online*, National Archives, accessed June 24, 2019, https://founders.archives.gov/documents/Adams/99 -02-02-6371.

11. Karl D. Jackson and Giovanna Maria Dora Dore, "A Republic If You Can Keep It," *American Interest*, September 15, 2016, https://www.the-american-interest.com/2016 /09/15/a-republic-if-you-can-keep-it (italics added).

12. Democracy Fund Voter Study Group, "Follow the Leader, Exploring American Support for Democracy and Authoritarianism," 2018, 11.

13. Ibid.

14. "1593, Benjamin Franklin," Respectfully Quoted: A Dictionary of Quotations. 1989, accessed June 3, 2019, https:// www.bartleby.com/73/1593.html.

LESSON 1: AMERICA ENLIGHTENED OR AUTHORITARIAN?

1. American Survey Research Project, "Three National Panel Surveys" fielded in the United States in October 2016, March 2017, and July 2017 by YouGov.

2. *Dred Scott v. Sandford*, 60 U.S. (19 How.) 393 (1857), dissent by Justice Curtis.

3. Abraham Lincoln, "A House Divided," in *The Collected Works of Abraham Lincoln Volume II*, ed. Roy P. Basler et al. (New Brunswick, NJ: Rutgers University Press, 1953), 147.

4. Ibid.

5. American Survey Research Project, "Three National Panel Surveys" fielded in the United States in October 2016, March 2017, and July 2017 by YouGov.

6. "Homecoming Speech at Chicago, Stephen A. Douglas, July 9, 1958," Great American Debates, Teaching American History, accessed August 10, 2019, https://teachingamericanhistory .org/library/document/homecoming-speech-at-chicago/.

7. Abraham Lincoln, "Speech at Chicago, Illinois," in *The*

Collected Works of Abraham Lincoln Volume II, ed. Roy P. Basler et al. (New Brunswick, NJ: Rutgers University Press, 1953), 501.

8. Eric Foner, *The Fiery Trial: Abraham Lincoln and American Slavery* (New York: W. W. Norton, 2010), 103.

9. Abraham Lincoln Historical Society, http://www.abraham -lincoln-history.org/lincoln-and-douglas-race-to-the -senate/.

10. Abraham Lincoln, "To Albert G. Hodges," in *The Collected Works of Abraham Lincoln Volume II*, ed. Roy P. Basler (New Brunswick, NJ: Rutgers University Press, 1953), 281.

11. Abraham Lincoln, "Speech at Springfield, Illinois," in *The Collected Works of Abraham Lincoln Volume II*, ed. Roy P. Basler et al. (New Brunswick, NJ: Rutgers University Press, 1953), 398–410.

12. Ibid.

13. American Survey Research Project, "Three National Panel Surveys" fielded in the United States in October 2016, March 2017, and July 2017 by YouGov.

LESSON 2: FOMENTING FEAR

1. Richard Hofstadter, "The Paranoid Style in American Politics," *Harper's Magazine* 229 (November 1964), 77–86, https://harpers.org/archive/1964/11/the-paranoid-style-in -american-politics/.

2. "Federalist 63, The Senate Continued," The Federalist Papers, Congress.gov Resources, accessed June 12, 2019, https://www.congress.gov/resources/display/content /The+Federalists+Papers.

3. "Public Troubled by 'Deep State'," Monmouth University Polling Institute, accessed September 13, 2019, https://www .monmouth.edu/polling-institute/reports/monmouthpoll _us_031918.

4. "The Duty of Americans at the Present Crisis by Timothy Dwight (July 4, 1798)," ConSource, accessed September 19, 2019, https://www.consource.org/document/the-duty-of -americans-at-the-present-crisis-by-timothy-dwight-1798-7 -4/.

5. Hofstadter, "Paranoid Style," 79–81 (quoting an unnamed Protestant militant).

6. Ibid.

7. Ibid., 80.

8. Abraham Lincoln, "To Joshua F. Speed," in *The Collected Works of Abraham Lincoln Volume II*, ed. Roy P. Basler et al. (New Brunswick, NJ: Rutgers University Press, 1953), 320–23.

9. Hofstadter, "Paranoid Style," 79–81.

10. "Speech of Joseph McCarthy, Wheeling, West Virginia, February 9, 1950," History Matters, accessed September 30, 2019, https://www.historymatters.gmu.edu/d/6456. As we will see, two days later the number of State Department employees on McCarthy's list had dwindled to fifty-seven, and the list was never made public.

11. Hofstadter, "Paranoid Style," 82.

12. "Trump's Full Inauguration Speech Transcript, Annotated," *Washington Post*, accessed September 30, 2019, https://www.washingtonpost.com/news/the-fix/wp/2017/01/20/donald-trumps-full-inauguration-speech-transcript-annotated/.

13. Hofstadter, "Paranoid Style," 82.

14. "Trump's Full Inauguration Speech."

15. Hofstadter, "Paranoid Style," 82.

16. "Trump's Full Inauguration Speech."

17. Hofstadter, "Paranoid Style," 83.

18. "Trump's Full Inauguration Speech."

19. Ibid.

LESSON 3: ALL LIES MATTER

1. "Federalist 63, The Senate Continued," The Federalist Papers, Congress.gov Resources, accessed June 12, 2019, https://www.congress.gov/resources/display/content/The+Federalists+Papers.

2. Ibid., Congress.gov Resources, Federalist 10 ("factious combinations").

3. Congress.gov Resources, Federalist 9; Robert Kagan, "This Is How Fascism Comes to America," Order from Chaos,

Brookings, accessed September 22, 2019, https://www
.brookings.edu/blog/order-from-chaor/2016/05/22/this-is
-how-fascism-comes-to-america/.

4. "Belief in Conspiracies Largely Depends on Political Identity,"
YouGov, December 27, 2016, accessed July 19, 2019, https://
today.yougov.com/topics/politics/articles-reports/2016/12/27
/belief-conspiracies-largely-depends-political-iden.

5. "Mobile Fact Sheet," Internet & Technology, Pew Research
Center, last modified June 12, 2019, https://pewresearch
.org/internet/fact-sheet/mobile/.

6. See Donald I. Warren, *Radio Priest: Charles Coughlin, the
Father of Hate Radio* (New York: Free Press, 1996).

7. Ibid., 28; Ruth Mugglebee, *Father Coughlin, the Radio
Priest of the Shrine of the Little Flower* (Garden City, NY:
Garden City Publishing, 1933), 184.

8. Louis B. Ward, *Father Charles E. Coughlin: An Authorized
Biography* (Detroit: Tower, 1933), 32.

9. Mugglebee, *Father Coughlin*, 357, as quoted in Bradley W.
Hart, *Hitler's American Friends: The Third Reich's Supporters in the United States* (New York: Thomas Dunne Books,
2018), 77.

10. Born in Canada, Father Coughlin could not run for president.

11. Hart, *Hitler's American Friends*, 86.

12. "Golden Hour Recording from November 20, 1938," Liber-
tyFight.com, accessed October 2, 2019, https://archive.org
/details/Father_Coughlin/FatherCoughlin_1938-11-20.mp3.

13. Hart, *Hitler's American Friends*, 70.

14. "TALKERS Estimetrix," Talkers.com, accessed November
10, 2019, www.talkers.com/top-talk-audiences/.

15. "Adams' Argument for the Defense: 3–4 December 1770,"
Founders Online, National Archives, September 15, 2019,
https://founders.archives.gov/documents/Adams/05-03-02
-0001-0004-0016.

16. Ruth Marcus, "Welcome to the Post-Truth Presidency," *Washington Post*, December 2, 2016, https://www.washingtonpost
.com/opinions/welcome-to-the-post-truth-presidency/2016
/12/02/.

17. Eric Bradner, "Conway: Trump White House Offered

'Alternative Facts' on Crowd Size," CNN, January 23, 2017, https://www.cnn/com/2017/01/22/politics/kellyanne-conway -alternative-facts/index.html.

18. "Trump Impeachment Hearing: Fiona Hill and David Holmes Testify in Impeachment Probe—11/21/2019," CNBC Television, last modified November 21, 2019, https://www.youtube .com/watch?v=GTh85DvUp_4.

19. Erich Fromm, *Escape from Freedom* (New York: Holt Paperback, 1994), 5.

20. Ibid., 249–50.

LESSON 4: GAGGING THE PRESS, QUASHING DISSENT

1. James C. Humes, "The Nation's First Civil Disobedient," *ABA Journal 58*, no. 3 (March 1972): 259.

2. "Indictment Against Thomas Cooper," National Archives and Records Administration, Records of the District Courts of the United States, Record Group 21, National Archives at Philadelphia, PA. National Archives Identifier 278969.

3. "Newspaper Broadside Filed in *United States v. Thomas Cooper*," November 5, 1799, National Archives, https:// www.docsteach.org/documents/document/newspaper -broadside-cooper.

4. American Survey Research Project, "Three National Panel Surveys" fielded in the United States in October 2016, March 2017, and July 2017 by YouGov.

5. "Transcript of Alien and Sedition Acts (1798)," www .ourdocuments.gov, accessed October 21, 2019, https://www .ourdocuments.gov/docphp?flash=false&doc=16&page =transcript.

6. Constitution of the United States, Amendment I (1791); Bruce A. Ragsdale, "The Sedition Act Trials," Federal Trials and Great Debates in United States History, Federal Judicial History Office, Federal Judicial Center, 2005, 1, https://www.fjc.gov/sites/default/files/trials/seditionacts .pdf.

7. Partisan politics, suspicions about the loyalties of some Democratic-Republicans, and fears of war with France were the troika of concerns behind the passage of the Sedition Act.

8. Ragsdale, "Sedition Act," 1.

9. Ibid., 1.

10. Ibid., 5.

11. Thomas Cooper, *"An Account of the Trial of Thomas Cooper of Northumberland on a Charge of Libel Against the President of the United States,"* Internet Archive, accessed September 20, 2019, https://archive.org/details/DKCOO17 /page/n61/mode/2up (see p. 20).

12. Ibid., preface.

LESSON 5: TAKING WHAT IS RIGHTFULLY OURS

1. Reply by Cherokee Nation to Secretary of War John C. Calhoun, in Thurman Wilkins, *Cherokee Tragedy: The Ridge Family and the Decimation of a People* (Norman: University of Oklahoma Press, 1986), 155. Calhoun, who later became a senator and vice president of the United States, had demanded the Cherokee renounce their national sovereignty and recognize the dominion of the state of Georgia, or leave the state at once.

2. Greenberg Quinlan Rosner Research, *Reclaiming Native Truth: A Project to Dispel America's Myths and Misconceptions* (Washington, DC: GQRR, 2018), 52.

3. Reginald Horsman, *Race and Manifest Destiny: The Origins of American Racial Anglo-Saxonism* (Boston: Harvard University Press, 1986), 195–96.

4. Samuel Carter III, *Cherokee Sunset: A Nation Betrayed* (Garden City, NY: Doubleday, 1976), 83.

5. "Transcript of President Andrew Jackson's Message to Congress 'On Indian Removal' (1830)," www.ourdocuments.gov, accessed September 25, 2019, https://www.ourdocuments .gov/docphp?flash=false&doc=25&page=transcript; "A Compilation of the Messages and Papers of the Presidents," edited by James C. Richardson, Volume III, Part 1, Project Gutenberg, accessed September 26, 2019, https://onlinebooks .library.upenn.edu/webbin/metabook?id=mppresidents.

6. Charles C. Royce, *The Cherokee Nation of Indians* (Whitefish, MT: Kessinger Legacy Reprints, Kessinger Publishing's Rare Reprints, 2010), 175.

7. Indian Removal Act, Public Law 21-148.

8. Henry Clay, "Correspondence to Daniel Webster, June 7, 1830," in *The Papers of Daniel Webster Volume III, Correspondence*, ed. Charles M. Wilste et al. (Hanover, NH: University Press of New England, 1974–88), 80–82.

9. *Worcester v. Georgia*, 31 U.S. (6 Pet.) 515 (1832).

10. Charles Warren, *The Supreme Court in United States History, Volume II* (Boston: Little, Brown, 1922), 219.

11. American Survey Research Project, "Three National Panel Surveys" fielded in the United States in October 2016, March 2017, and July 2017 by YouGov.

12. J. W. Powell, Director, *The Fifth Annual Report of the Bureau of Ethnology to the Secretary of the Smithsonian Institution, 1883–1884* (Washington, DC: Government Printing Office: 1887), 284–85.

13. Carter, *Cherokee Sunset*, 211. (Quote from a volunteer from Georgia who enlisted in one of the military units ordered to remove the Cherokee.)

14. Letter from the Reverend Evan Jones in *Baptist Missionary Magazine*, vol. XVIII, 236, quoted in Grant Foreman, *Indian Removal: The Emigration of the Five Civilized Tribes of Indians* (Norman: University of Oklahoma Press, 1932), 288–89.

15. "December 3, 1838: Second Annual Message to Congress," Miller Center, University of Virginia, accessed September 24, 2019, https://millercenter.org/the-presidency/presidential-speeches/december-3-1838.

16. Theodore Roosevelt, *The Winning of the West* (American Cowboy Books, 2014), Kindle edition, 126–30.

17. Stephen Breyer, *Making Our Democracy Work: A Judge's View* (New York: Alfred A. Knopf, 2010), 30.

18. Warren, *Supreme Court*, 216.

LESSON 6: USING FEAR AND VIOLENCE TO CONTROL AND SUBORDINATE OTHERS

1. Justice for Victims of Lynching Act, S. 3178 (2018), Section 2, Findings (3). A recent report on lynching reports that "at least" an additional "2,000 Black women, men, and children were victims of racial terror lynchings" between 1865

and 1876. "Reconstruction In America: Racial Violence After the Civil War, 1865-1876," Equal Justice Initiative, https://eji.org/report/reconstruction-in-america/.

2. Equal Justice Initiative, *Lynching in America: Confronting the Legacy of Racial Terror, Second Edition, Report Summary* (Montgomery, AL: Equal Justice Initiative, 2015), 5.

3. Justice for Victims of Lynching Act, S. 488 (2019), Section 2, Findings (3).

4. Ida B. Wells-Barnett, *On Lynchings* (Mineola, NY: Dover, 2014), 81.

5. Ibid., 53.

6. Ibid., 82.

7. Ibid., 59.

8. Ibid., 86.

9. Justice for Victims of Lynching Act, S. 488 (2019), Section 2, Findings (5).

10. Justice for Victims of Lynching Act, S. 3178 (2018), Section 2, Findings (1).

11. The number of lynchings recorded in 1890 was ninety-six.

12. Ida B. Wells-Barnett labeled lynching America's "national crime" in a speech delivered in Chicago in 1900. See Ida B. Wells, "Lynch Law in America," BlackPast, https://www.blackpast.org/african-american-history/1900-ida-b-wells-lynch-law-america/.

13. From *Theodore Roosevelt and His Time, Shown in His Own Letters*, ed. Joseph Bishop (1920), quoted in Williams L. Ziglar, "The Decline of Lynching in America," *International Social Science Review* 63, no. 1 (Winter 1988): 17.

14. In his 1897 inaugural address, President McKinley also denounced lynching. As president, he took no action to curtail it.

15. President Theodore Roosevelt, "State of the Union Address: Theodore Roosevelt (December 3, 1906)," Infoplease, accessed October 24, 2019, https://www.infoplease.com/primary-sources/government/presidential-speeches/state-union-address-theodore-roosevelt-december-3-1906.

16. Ibid.

17. Quoted in Stacy Pratt McDermott, "'An Outrageous Proceeding': A Northern Lynching and the Enforcement of

Anti-Lynching Legislation in Illinois, 1905–1910," *Journal of Negro History* 84, no. 1 (Winter 1999): 71.

18. Ida B. Wells-Barnett, *On Lynchings*, 83.

19. "Lynching Statistics from Tuskegee Institute, 1882–1968," Internet Archive, accessed September 27, 2019, https://archive.org/details/tuskegeelynchingstatistics.

20. After 1922, the number of public murders by mob decreased steadily.

21. "John Hartfield Will Be Lynched by Ellisville Mob at 5 O'clock This Afternoon," *Daily News* (Jackson, MS), June 26, 1919, 1.

22. The Dyer anti-lynching bill passed the House of Representatives on January 26, 1922.

23. Justin McCarthy, "Gallup Vault: 72% Support for Anti-Lynching Bill in 1937," Gallup Vault, Gallup, accessed October 11, 2019, https://news.gallup.com/vault/234371/gallup-vault-support-anti-lynching-bill-1937.aspx.

24. Justice for Victims of Lynching Act, S. 3178 (2018).

25. "U.S. Passes First Anti-Lynching Law After Senate Vote," BBC News, December 20, 2018, accessed October 11, 2019, https://bbc.com/news/world-us-canada-46634184.

LESSON 7: THE DRIVING OUT

1. "Dots and Dashes, the Chinese Bill a Law," *Dillon Tribune*, May 12, 1882.

2. American Survey Research Project, "Three National Panel Surveys" fielded in the United States in October 2016, March 2017, and July 2017 by YouGov.

3. "California Constitution of 1879, Article XIX: Chinese, Section 1," California State Polytechnic University, Pomona, accessed November, 3, 2019, hyyps://www.cpp.edu/~jlkorey/calcon1879.pdf. (Full quote: "Chinese: Section 1. The Legislature shall prescribe all necessary regulations for the protection of the State, and the counties, cities, and towns thereof, from the burdens and evils arising from the presence of aliens who are or may become vagrants, paupers, mendicants, criminals, or invalids afflicted with contagious or infectious diseases, and from aliens otherwise

dangerous or detrimental to the well-being or peace of the State, and to impose conditions upon which persons may reside in the state, and to provide means and mode of their removal from the State, upon failure or refusal to comply with such conditions.")

4. Congressman Albert Willis, "Debate on H.R. 5804, the Chinese Exclusion Act of 1882," *Congressional Record*, April 17, 1882.

5. Senator Wilkinson Call, "Debate on H.R. 5804, the Chinese Exclusion Act of 1882," *Congressional Record*, April 28, 1882.

6. Senator George H. Pendleton, "Debate on H.R. 5804, the Chinese Exclusion Act of 1882," *Congressional Record*, April 28, 1882.

7. American Survey Research Project, "Three National Panel Surveys" fielded in the United States in October 2016, March 2017, and July 2017 by YouGov.

8. Jean Pfaelzer, *Driven Out: The Forgotten War Against Chinese Americans* (Berkeley: University of California Press, 2007), ix.

9. Ibid., 261.

10. "The Massacre of the Chinese: Sixteen Known to Have Been Killed and Many Wounded," *New York Times*, September 5, 1885.

11. Pfaelzer, *Driven Out*, 261.

12. Ibid., xviii.

13. American Survey Research Project, "Three National Panel Surveys" fielded in the United States in October 2016, March 2017, and July 2017 by YouGov.

14. Jason Silverstein, "Trump's Top Immigration Official Reworks the Words on the Statue of Liberty," CBS News, August 14, 2019 (italics added).

LESSON 8: FEAR AS A PATH TO POWER

1. Quoted in Roberta Strauss Feuerlicht, *America's Reign of Terror: World War I, the Red Scare, and the Palmer Raids* (New York: Random House, 1971), 32.

2. Sworn Affidavit of Mitchel Lavrowsky, exhibit 2b, "Report

upon the Illegal Practices of the United States Department of Justice," National Popular Government League, Internet Archive, May 1920, accessed December 3, 2019, https://archive.org/details/toamericanpeople00natiuoft.

3. American Survey Research Project, "Three National Panel Surveys" fielded in the United States on October 2016, March 2017, and July 2017 by YouGov.

4. "Exhibit 2, Report upon the Illegal Practices of the United States Department of Justice," National Popular Government League, Internet Archive, accessed December 3, 2019, https://archive.org/details/toamericanpeople00natiuoft.

5. Ibid.

6. "Exhibit 1, Report upon the Illegal Practices of the United States Department of Justice," National Popular Government League, Internet Archive, accessed December 3, 2019, https://archive.org/details/toamericanpeople00natiuoft.

7. "Palmer Declares Alien 'Reds' Are to Be Deported," *Ogden Standard*, November 8, 1919, 1. The number of cities where the test raids were conducted is disputed, ranging from a few to as many as nineteen.

8. Ibid.

9. Ibid.

10. "Editorial: The Red Assassins," *Washington Post*, January 4, 1920.

11. The "slacker raid" occurred in September 1918 and involved hundreds of Department of Justice agents and NYPD officers as well as a reported 2,000 American Protective League vigilantes.

12. A. Mitchell Palmer, "The Case Against the 'Reds'," *Forum* 63, no. 2 (February 1920): 63–75.

13. John Braeman, "World War One and the Crisis of American Liberty," *American Quarterly* 16, no. 1 (Spring 1964): 108.

14. "3,000 Arrested in Nation-Wide Round-Up of 'Reds'; Palmer Directs Raids in 35 Cities; 650 Seized Here," *New York Tribune*, January 3, 1920, 1.

15. Frederick R. Barkley, "Jailing Radicals in Detroit," *The Nation*, January 2, 1920.

16. "Exhibit 5, Report upon the Illegal Practices of the United

States Department of Justice," National Popular Government League, Internet Archive, accessed December 3, 2019, https://archive.org/details/toamericanpeople00natiuoft.

17. *New York Call*, April 26, 1920, as quoted in Donald Johnson, "The Political Career of A. Mitchell Palmer," *Pennsylvania History: A Journal of Mid-Atlantic Studies* 25, no. 4 (October 1958): 346.

18. "May Death Plot Is Uncovered," *Tulsa Daily World*, April 30, 1920, 1.

19. "No May Day Outbreaks in U.S.," *New York Tribune*, May 2, 1920, 1.

20. "Introduction: Report upon the Illegal Practices of the United States Department of Justice," National Popular Government League, Internet Archive, accessed December 3, 2019, https://archive.org/details/toamericanpeople00natiuoft.

21. Braeman, "Crisis of American Liberty," 109.

22. Michael Lipka, "Muslims and Islam: Key Findings in the U.S. and Around the World," Fact Tank, Pew Research Center, August 9, 2017, https://www.pewresearch.org/fact-tank/2017/08/09/muslims-and-islam-key-findings-in-the-u-s-and-around-the-world/.

LESSON 9: GALVANIZING GROUP IDENTITY

1. Daniel Greene and Frank Newport, "American Public Opinion and the Holocaust," Polling Matters, Gallup, April 23, 2018, https://news.gallup.com/opinion/polling-matters/232949/american-public-opinion-holocaust.aspx.

2. This first-person remembrance of the Anschluss recorded and posted online in 2016 in response to comments by the neo-fascist leader of the Austrian Freedom Party is particularly disturbing: "When they made Jews clean the streets, the people of Vienna stood there ... men and women ... watched and laughed. 'Look at that. Haha ... that was funny.' I experienced a civil war as a seven-year-old and I've never forgotten it. It was the first time I saw dead bodies; regrettably, not the last. . . . Yah ... I've never forgotten it. It buried itself so deep in me." Elizabeth Roberts, "Holocaust

Survivor Pleads with Austrian Voters: Don't Let Far Right Win," CNN, December 1, 2016, https://edition.cnn.com /2016/11/30/europe/austria-election-holocaust-survivor -plea.

LESSON 10: SILENCE OF THE LAW

1. "Republicans Uneasy with Concept of Executive Orders, but Support Some Specific Ones," Politics & Current Affairs, *Economist*/YouGov Poll, January 25, 2016, https://d25d2506sfb94s.cloudfront.net/cumulus_uploads /document/ps6zskmuwy/econTabReport.pdf (p. 137, table 127).

2. George Takei, "From 'George Takei on challenging the "mindless inhumanity" of U.S. history's darker chapters,'" interview with Judy Woodruff, *PBS NewsHour*, October 23, 2019, https://www.pbs.org.newshour/show/george-takei-on -challenging-the-mindless-inhumanity-of-u-s-historys-darker- chapters.

3. Ibid.

4. George and his brother also carried two small suitcases.

5. George Takei, "'At Least During the Internment . . .' Are Words I Thought I'd Never Utter," *Foreign Policy*, June 19, 2018.

6. Around 16,000 Japanese, German, Italian, and other aliens were arrested by the FBI. Most of them were released.

7. Francis Biddle, *In Brief Authority* (Garden City, NY: Doubleday, 1962), 207.

8. *Oakland Tribune*, December 13, 1941, quoted in Gerald Stanley, "Justice Deferred: A Fifty-Year Perspective on Japanese-Internment Historiography," *Southern California Quarterly* 74, no. 2 (Summer 1992): 182.

9. *Congressional Record* (Appendix), December 8, 1941, A5554, quoted in Stanley, "Justice Deferred," 182.

10. Stanley, "Justice Deferred," 192.

11. Eric J. Sundquist, "The Japanese-American Internment: A Reappraisal," *American Scholar* 57, no. 4 (Autumn 1988): 542.

12. Ibid., 539.

13. Bill Hosokawa, *Nisei, the Quiet Americans: The Story of a People* (Boulder: University Press of Colorado, 1969), 287–88.

14. Mikiso Hane, "Wartime Internment," *Journal of American History* 77, no. 2 (September 1990): 571.

15. Stanley, "Justice Deferred," 191.

16. Executive Order 9066, issued February 19, 1942, President Franklin Roosevelt.

17. Noah Feldman, *Scorpions: The Battles and Triumphs of FDR's Great Supreme Court Justices* (New York: Twelve, 2010), 239.

18. Loyalty testing of Japanese Americans began more than a year later, after they were interned.

19. Stanley, "Justice Deferred," 192.

20. Ibid., 181.

21. "Gallup Vault: WWII—Era Support for Japanese Internment," Art Swift, Gallup Vault, August 31, 2016, https://news.gallup.com/vault/195257/gallup-vault-wwii-era-support-japanese-internment.aspx.

22. Mark Tushnet, ed., *I Dissent: Great Opposing Opinions in Landmark Supreme Court Cases* (Boston: Beacon Press, 2008), 114.

23. *Korematsu v. United States*, 323 U.S. 214 (1944), dissent by Justice Frank Murphy; the same day *Korematsu* was decided, the Court ruled on *Ex parte Mitsuye Endo*, another detention case. In *Endo*, the Court ruled not on the constitutionality of exclusion and detainment but on the meaning of Roosevelt's executive order. It concluded that Executive Order 9066 did not allow for the detention of loyal Americans. Mitsuye Endo and others who could prove their loyalty to the United States had to be freed. The *Endo* decision was a fig leaf that provided little cover for the Court's rewrite of the Constitution in *Korematsu*, a landmark ruling. *Endo* interpreted a time-bound presidential order about internment camps that were already scheduled for closure.

24. "President Reagan's Remarks at the Japanese American Internment Compensation Bill Signing on August 10, 1988," https://en.wikipedia.org/wiki/File:President_Reagan%27s

_at_the_Japanese-American_Internment_Compensation
_Bill_signing_on_August_10,_1988.webm.

25. Ibid.

26. Ilya Somin, "Justice Scalia on Kelo and Korematsu," *The Volokh Conspiracy* (blog), *Washington Post*, February 8, 2014, https://www.washingtonpost.com.

27. Kavitha George, "Trump's Family Separation Policy Is Child Abuse, According to the UN Human Rights Chief," *Bustle*, June 18, 2018, https://www.bustle.com/p/trumps -family-separation-policy-is child-abuse-according-to-the -un-human-rights-chief-9455171.

28. Quinnipiac University Poll, June 18, 2018, https://poll .qu.edu/national/release-detail?ReleaseID=2550.

29. Mary Louise Kelly, "Looking at Lasting Effects of Trump's Family Separation Policy at the Southern Border," *All Things Considered*, NPR, January 1, 2020, htpps://www .npr.org/2020/01/01/792916538/looking-at-lasting-effects -of-trumps-family-separation-policy-at-the-southern-bo.

LESSON 11: FEAR BREEDS REPRESSION; REPRESSION BREEDS HATE; HATE MENACES STABLE GOVERNMENT

1. David M. Oshinsky, *A Conspiracy So Immense: The World of Joe McCarthy* (New York: Free Press, 1983), 54.

2. "Gallup Vault: Celebrity Witnesses Before Congress in 1947," RJ Reinhart, Gallup Vault, April 12, 2018, https:// news.gallup.com/vault/232430/gallup-vault-celebrity- witnesses-congress-1947.aspx.

3. Hiss maintained his innocence throughout the hearings in 1948 but was convicted on two counts of perjury two years later. HUAC chairman Rep. Thomas suffered a similar fate. Accused of fraud by none other than legendary columnist Jack Anderson, he resigned from Congress in January 1950 and was sentenced to eighteen months in prison.

4. Joseph McCarthy, "'Enemies from Within' Speech Deliv- ered in Wheeling, West Virginia (1950)," https://liberalarts .utexas.edu/coretexts/_files/resources/texts/1950%20Mc Carthy%20Enemies.pdf.

5. Ibid.

6. Ibid.

7. Quoted in Oshinsky, *Conspiracy*, 114.

8. "Timeline of Polling History: People That Shaped the United States, and the World," The Gallup Poll: 65 Years of Polling History, https://news.gallup.com/poll/9964/Timeline -Polling-History-People-Shaped-United-States-World.aspx (See 1950).

9. Oshinsky, *Conspiracy*, 143.

10. "Declaration of Conscience," Margaret Chase Smith, June 1, 1950 (delivered), "American Rhetoric: Top 100 Speeches," https://www.americanrhetoric.com/speeches/margaret chasesmithconscience.html.

11. Robert Shogan, *No Sense of Decency* (Chicago: Ivan R. Dee, 2009), 226.

LESSON 12: THE SURVEILLANCE SOCIETY AND THE BIG LIE

1. "What Americans Think About NSA Surveillance, National Security and Privacy," George Gao, Pew Research Center, May 29, 2015, https://www.pewresearch.org/fact -tank/2015/05/29/what-americans-think-about-nsa -surveillance-national-security-and-privacy/.

2. Presidential Proclamation, "Declaration of National Emergency by Reason of Certain Terrorist Attacks," September 14, 2001; Executive Order, "Ordering the Ready Reserve of the Armed Forces to Active Duty and Delegating Certain Authorities to the Secretary of Defense and the Secretary of Transportation," September 14, 2001; Executive Order, "Establishing the Office of Homeland Security and the Homeland Security Council," October 8, 2001; James Risen and Eric Lichtblau, "Bush Lets U.S. Spy on Callers Without Courts," *New York Times*, December 16, 2005.

3. Gina Marie Stevens, *Report for Congress, Privacy: Total Information Awareness Programs and Related Information Access, Collection and Protection Laws*, Congressional Research Service, The Library of Congress, updated March 21, 2003.

4. Amy Belasco, "Total Information Awareness Programs:

Funding, Composition, and Oversight Issues," quoted in Newton Lee, *Counterterrorism and Cybersecurity: Total Information Awareness*, 2nd ed. (Cham, Switzerland: Springer International, 2015), 138.

5. Stevens, "Privacy," CRS-2.

6. Ibid.

7. John Markoff, "Pentagon Plans a Computer System That Would Peek at Personal Data of Americans," *New York Times*, November 9, 2002.

8. "Stunning New Report on Domestic NSA Dragnet Spying Confirms ACLU Surveillance Warnings," American Civil Liberties Union, last modified March 12, 2008, htpps://aclu.org/press-releases/stunning-new-report-domestic-nsa-dragnet-spying-confirms-acle-surveillance-warnings.

9. Mark William Pontin, "The Total Information Awareness Project Lives On," *MIT Technology Review*, April 26, 2006.

10. Fourth Amendment to the U.S. Constitution.

CONCLUSION

1. Rogers M. Smith, "Beyond Tocqueville, Myrdal, and Hartz: The Multiple Traditions in America," *American Political Science Review* 87, no. 3 (1993).

2. *Whitney v. California*, 275 U.S. 357 (1927), concurrence by Justice Brandeis (originally written as a true dissent in another case).

3. James Madison, "Parties," *National Gazette*, January 23, 1792, quoted in Stanley Elkins and Eric McKitrick, *The Age of Federalism: The Early American Republic, 1788–1800* (New York: Oxford University Press, 1993), 266.

4. Margaret Chase Smith, "Declaration of Conscience," June 1, 1950, https://www.americanrhetoric.com/speeches/margaret chasesmithconscience.html.

APPENDIX 2

1. Marc J. Hetherington and Jonathan D. Weiler, *Authoritarianism and Polarization in American Politics* (Cambridge: Cambridge University Press, 2009), 36.

APPENDIX 3

1. In his famous *The Crooked Timber of Humanity: Chapters in the History of Ideas*, ed. Henry Hardy (Princeton, NJ: Princeton University Press, 2013), Isaiah Berlin argues that "Maistre's famous, terrible vision of life . . . has an affinity with the paranoiac world of modern Fascism, which is startling to find so early in the nineteenth century."

2. Isaiah Berlin, "Joseph de Maistre and the Origins of Fascism," in *The Crooked Timber of Humanity*, ed. Henry Hardy (Princeton, NJ: Princeton University Press, 2013), 95–177.

3. Ibid.

4. Ibid.

5. Ibid.

6. Ibid.

7. Ibid.

8. Ibid.

9. Ibid.

10. Erich Fromm, *Escape from Freedom* (New York: Farrar and Rinehart, 1941), 53.

11. Ibid., 2.

12. Ibid., 74.

13. Franz Samelson, "The Authoritarian Character from Berlin to Berkeley and Beyond: The Odyssey of a Problem," in *Strength and Weakness: The Authoritarian Personality Today*, ed. William F. Stone, Gerda Lederer, and Richard Christie (New York: Springer, 1993), 22.

14. Many researchers do not include "don't know" as an answer with each pair. It is excluded for two very good reasons. First, excluding "don't know" avoids a statistical problem called variance. When "don't know" is omitted as an answer option, the meaning of the child-rearing questions appears to be invariant between different racial groups in the United States. In this case, invariance is good. It means, for example, that white and black Americans have similar understandings of paired attributes. Second, the binary option replicates real political choices people are compelled to make when voting or choosing which side in a political debate to support.

15. Marc J. Hetherington and Jonathan D. Weiler, *Authoritarianism and Polarization in American Politics* (Cambridge: Cambridge University Press, 2009), 48.

16. Ibid.

17. Karen Stenner, *The Authoritarian Dynamic* (Cambridge: Cambridge University Press, 2003), 24.

18. From a Geert Wilders flyer distribution event in Breda, the Netherlands, to a hotel conference room just off I-75 in Monroe County, Pennsylvania, I talked with or listened to nearly 200 dispositional authoritarians over the course of a year.

19. John Duckitt, "Authoritarianism and Group Identification: A New View of an Old Construct," *Political Psychology* 10, no. 1 (March 1989): 63–84.

20. The countries include the United States, the Netherlands, France, Germany, Austria, and Italy.

21. Paul Rosenberg, "Don't Think of a Rampaging Elephant: Linguist George Lakoff Explains How the Democrats Helped Elect Trump," *Salon*, January 15, 2017, http://www.salon.com/2017/01/15/dont-think-of-a-rampaging-elephant-linguist-george-lakoff-explains-how-the-democrats-helped-elect-trump/.

INDEX

ABOUT THE AUTHOR

Leah K. Glasheen

MATTHEW C. MACWILLIAMS is a scholar, an award-winning practitioner of American politics, and a recognized expert on authoritarianism. He was the first researcher to use survey research to establish a link between Trump's core supporters and authoritarianism. Early in the Republican nominating contest for president in 2015, he warned that Trump's activation of American authoritarians would make his candidacy virtually unstoppable. His articles on Trump in *Politico* and *Vox* and on the London School of Economics blog sparked an international media debate that contributed to the framing of Trump and his tactics as authoritarian. His work was reprinted or referenced by leading media around the world, including CNN, MSNBC, ABC, NBC, CBS, *The Washington Post*, *Newsweek*, *New York Times* columnist David Brooks, NPR, *The Atlantic*, and *Der Spiegel*. He has presented to elected officials and civil society leaders in the United States and Europe about the rise of authoritarianism and its implications for the future of democracy.